GO PROVE SOMETHING!

A BASKETBALL PLAYER'S GUIDE TO LEGALLY USING PEDs

GO PROVE SOMETHING!

A BASKETBALL PLAYER'S GUIDE TO LEGALLY USING PEDs

BY ANTHONY M. DRAGO

FOREWORD BY LEE TAFT

MAURICE BASSETT

books for athletes of the mind

Go Prove Something! A Basketball Players Guide to Legally Using PEDs

Maurice Bassett
P.O. Box 839
Anna Maria, FL 34216-0839

MauriceBassett@gmail.com
www.MauriceBassett.com

Illustrations by David Michael Moore
Cover design by Colleen Raney
Cover photos by Katiejo Kardel
Editing and interior layout by Chris Nelson

ISBN: 978-1-60025-093-4

Library of Congress Control Number: 2016934392

First Edition

What People Are Saying About Anthony M. Drago

In Drago's highly-motivating book, basketball becomes a powerful metaphor for life itself. A book every player and player's family should own!

~ **Steve Chandler**, *Author*, Crazy Good: A Book of CHOICES

Anthony Drago is as genuine a person as I have met in basketball. He has as much heart as any coach I've played for and he puts it into what he does for other people. He is all about believing in having your spirit right, and what that can do for yourself and others in whatever you do in this life. He's real with you.

~ **Steve Weingarten**, *Pro Basketball Player*

As an NBA Player Agent operating out of one the largest basketball facilities in the country, Basketball City, I deal with a lot of trainers. Anthony Drago is one of the best in the business. I can say that from personal experience, without hesitation. His approach is unique, his methods are tested and his professionalism is unwavering. I highly recommend that any players looking to take their games to the next level go see Anthony.

~ **BJ Bass**, *Owner, RBA Sports*

It is refreshing to read what's not only a how-to book but also a *why*-to book. Anthony addresses what every parent and player needs to know about having a Purpose, having Persistence and exhibiting Passion! This book is a must read for anyone at any level!

~ **John Saintignon**, *International Head Coach, former NCAA Pac-10 coach and guest speaker*

I coached Anthony when he was a teen and I honestly can't think of a more tenacious competitor of the game. Completely coach-able back then as in the present. What he has to share is a game changer—so grab a drink and a snack, and turn off your cell phone. *Go Prove Something! A Basketball Player's Guide to Legally Using PEDs* promises to deliver great insights. Enjoy.

~ **Nate Robinson**, *Author*

Anthony Drago is one of the best trainers I have had the pleasure to meet. His no-nonsense, "tell them what they need to know" approach is needed in today's progressive fitness industry. A certified trainer and student of human development for over twenty years, I have rarely if ever come across someone who puts as much care, time and thoughtful consideration into building out a comprehensive system to reach better health and wellness than Anthony Drago. He is a great value to the Inspire Sport, Better Life Through Sports program, as he will be to anyone who reads *Go Prove Something! A Basketball Player's Guide to Legally Using PEDs*.

~ **Andre Wade**, *Founder/CEO, Inspire Talent Brand Management*

Go Prove Something! A Basketball Player's Guide to Legally Using PEDs is essential for the mental preparation and physical excellence of this generation's young athletes. Anthony Drago has made it both simple and impactful for the reader to comprehend and to get the results they want at warp speed.

~ **Michael R. Carter**, *Financial & Sports Management Professional*

I've known Anthony for over fifteen years and his desire to help others is second to none. His business mind, coupled with his passion for life, make him a leader among leaders. This book is for anyone in any industry. If you want a better life, this book is a must read.

~ **Steve Carter**, *MLM Multi-Million Dollar Earner and Entrepreneur*

Anthony Drago has one of the most creative and interesting minds I have ever come across. He has the innate ability to connect with a diverse group of people. His ability to not only speak what he knows and believes but to actually live by it puts him head and shoulders above his competition. He also has the ability to put his own flair on the knowledge he obtains so that something that may be difficult for most can be simplified to where a child can understand it.

~ **Dami Sapara**, *Entrepreneur*

I have known Anthony for over fifteen years, and his approach to developing young athletes, both physically and mentally, is as unique, innovative and results driven as any I have seen. This book will literally change the lives of anyone who internalizes Anthony's message.

~ **Robert Smith**, *Father and Coach*

When it comes to success and preparing the mind I have not met anyone like Anthony Drago. He has helped me and many others train our minds to be successful at anything that we aspire to—and not just basketball. A true believer that anything and everything is possible.

~ **Michael Balogun**, *Future Pro Basketball Player*

I have known Anthony for over a quarter century. All that time Anthony has shown the kind of attention to detail that makes him proficient in everything he does, but more than this he has an extreme passion, dedication and no-quit attitude in everything he involves himself with. His love of mentoring and his thirst for knowledge to better himself is unmatched by anyone I know. Given his continuous competitive drive on top of all the abovementioned attributes, I'd have to seriously question your commitment to self-improvement and awareness if you didn't read *Go Prove Something! A Basketball Player's Guide to Legally Using PEDs*.

~ **Ronald D. James**, *Father, Coach and Entrepreneur*

Go Prove Something! A Basketball Player's Guide to Legally Using PEDs is a game changer. Every young basketball player needs a copy.

~ **Steven P. Guarnieri**, *Firefighter, NYC Fire Department*

It is quite evident that Mr. Drago certainly understands the power of the mind, as he so elegantly describes in his book *Go Prove Something! A Basketball Player's Guide to Legally Using PEDs*. I absolutely love the analogies the author uses to define the importance of and power in approaching everything you do in life with the appropriate mindset. In doing so, we can literally control our own destinies. This is a very strong and much needed message, not just for an aspiring basketball player looking to enhance their performance, but also for anyone looking to enhance everyday performance in their own lives. This book is a definite must-read.

~ **Dan Rooney**, *Author of* Kids Grow with Info: A Resource Guide for Kids, Parents & Educators, *Children's Financial Success Expert and Business Support Specialist*

Anthony "Yoda" Drago was the best training coach and motivator I ever had because his teachings went way beyond basketball. It wasn't about just preparing me to abandon bad habits but making sure I created and became accustomed to new ones. It wasn't about just learning how to move my body properly but how to properly move my life toward the right path. Sometimes I cried tears of joy and sometimes tears of pain. All of the sacrifices he made to make my time in New York enjoyable were appreciated then and will always be appreciated. You see those movies about people saving/changing other people's lives; Yoda really did that for me. And for that I will be forever grateful.

~ **Julien Bendeke**, *Microbiologist*

I had the pleasure of meeting Anthony Drago several years ago when he was on the Tottenville High School basketball team. At that time, he was a hardworking individual who demonstrated true leadership qualities. Fifteen years later he worked as a coach and mentor with my Shoot for Success basketball training program. He trained some of my top Division 1 players, which I believe helped get them to the next level. Through his experiences he has now been able to translate his journey in a captivating story to share with the world. I know *Go Prove Something! A Basketball Player's Guide to Legally Using PEDs* will be an inspirational story for anyone at any level. I am looking forward to reading it again because he has the tools to extract greatness from anyone open to receiving his powerful message.

~ **Gerry Mosley**, *Shoot for Success Founder & Coach*

My brother from another mother, Anthony Drago, is and will continue to be a person that stands out from the rest when it comes to developing our youth. His passion and attention to detail are unlike anything I have ever seen in the basketball world. I have traveled all over this country and worked with some of the top trainers and coaches out there, and the one thing I can say with complete conviction is that you would be hard pressed to find a more dedicated person than Anthony who is focused on developing our youth to be as successful off the court as they are on the court. That is why everyone needs a copy of *Go Prove Something! A Basketball Player's Guide to Legally Using PEDs*.

~ **Tony Devine**, *Creator of The Original Profender*

I recently had to privilege of reading *Go Prove Something! A Basketball Player's Guide to Legally Using PEDs* by Anthony Drago. This book is a slam dunk! Anthony is a premier basketball athletic skills coach, and his book has the basketball edge to it. But I don't care if you play another sport, are a businessman, or someone just wanting to change your life . . . This book is a must. Anthony does what most don't do when writing a book about sports: he addresses the mind, body, and skills needed to succeed. I highly recommend this book for students/athletes as well as coaches and trainers. The straightforward strategies Anthony uses will help you develop a roadmap to success!

~ **Lee Taft**, *Multi-Directional Speed Coach (www.leetaft.com)*

Go Prove Something! A Basketball Player's Guide to Legally Using PEDs is a refreshing, must read for all parents and young players who truly want to improve their games and reach for greatness. PEDs sound like drugs, but trust me: Anthony is not talking about an illegal substance but an approach to life and basketball that is both physical and mental. The Performance Enhancement Training road Anthony takes you down shows many unique insights and training methods that will definitely open your eyes. Anthony's desire to help others comes through so easily when reading this book. I am so glad I read it, and you should read it too.

~ **Ron Naclerio**, *Cardozo High School Boys Basketball Coach, most wins in NYC PSAL (over 723)*

Dedication

This book you hold in your hands is dedicated to my wonderful and amazing wife Dena and our son, Parker.

Dena, you have been by my side for over a decade. I love you more every day and sometimes it still feels like we are in the infatuation phase. You have been there to support me and keep me on course when I lose focus (which happens a lot). You have made me the man I am today and for that I am forever grateful. I truly cannot imagine my life without you. I thank you for being my better half and I love you.

Parker, you just turned two years old and it has honestly been the best two years of my life. Every day and night that I am privileged to be a part of your life is absolutely a blessing. Years from now you will read this and understand the unconditional love Mommy and I have for you. Understand that our family is everything to me and you have created a bond between us that can never be broken. Everything I do in my life is for you and Mommy. I love you more than life itself.

Nothing will ever be attempted, if all possible objections must be first overcome.

~ **Samuel Johnson**

Nothing will ever be attempted, if all possible objections must be first overcome.

~ **Samuel Johnson**

Contents

Foreword

by **Lee Taft**

It was a hot summer day in 1991 as I made my way to my first class as a graduate student in Daphne, Alabama. I was getting ready to attend a sports psychology class and had mixed emotions.

I loved sports psychology and was excited about what I would learn. At the same time, I was nervous about what my professor would be like; we've all have had the occasional professor or teacher who can make or break our classroom experience.

Well, five minutes into the class I was relieved and ramped up to learn a ton.

My professor was the sports psychologist for Florida State Athletics, and she was able to pique my interest from the opening bell.

Over my years of coaching I've used many of the principles and concepts she taught me. I still do, to this day. Not only did she do a great job of teaching me during the class, she also inspired me to continue learning about performance and how to improve it.

I eventually branched out into the study of helping athletes understand how powerful their decisions are. Their attitudes on and off the court and field shape most of their decisions. Put simply: decisions impact performance.

Fast forward many years. One day I received an email from a basketball performance coach named Anthony Drago. He was interested in learning more about my methods and how to advance in the profession. Although we never met face-to-face, we became good friends and acquired mutual respect for each other.

Anthony is what I call a "High Motor Guy." He's like the basketball player who never stops working. Over the years he and I have communicated about basketball and how to improve performance. We've also talked about the business side of the profession and the kinds of strategies that could help us get our message out to more people and create a bigger impact.

When he shared this book with me one thing became very clear: Anthony Drago is on a mission to change how we look at the development of basketball players.

He's realized that there is much more to becoming a better player than just improving the skills of the game. Anthony understands that all of our actions are directed by something seemingly simple, but often overlooked: *our decisions*!

As I read his book I was amazed at how his approach to improving a player's game was so much deeper than any I'd seen before. He hits on so many important areas of developing strong decision making, but most importantly he teaches us *how* to make those all-important decisions.

All coaches look for that edge, that perfect strategy . . . Frankly, all coaches are looking for the *answer*.

Go Prove Something! A Basketball Players Guide to Legally Using PEDs is that answer.

I know what you're thinking: PEDs are illegal drugs (<u>P</u>erformance <u>E</u>nhancing <u>D</u>rugs).

But I assure you they're not.

I'm not going to spoil the secret here, but I will let you in on something:

This book, without a doubt, is going to improve your basketball abilities—but if by the end you still think it's only about basketball, well . . . read it again!

In this book, Anthony addresses the importance of *complete* player development—not just how to play the game. He compares the process of building a house and all the work that goes into it with how an athlete develops his or her mind, body and skills.

Have you ever lived in a neighborhood where new homes were being built? I have, and once you get past the noise and the mud, it's really fascinating to watch the process unfolding. You see the foundation being laid, the frame going up, the essential systems (wiring, plumbing, etc.) put in place, and the roof set atop the house. Eventually each aspect of the home comes into place to meet a specific need.

Well, in a nutshell, Anthony uses this process as an analogy for how the development of a basketball player should occur. He cleverly takes us step-by-step through how an athlete needs to "build" their abilities: their mind, body, and skills, relating each one to a stage in the building of a house.

(And believe me: even though this book has "basketball" in the title, Anthony is helping *all* athletes.)

It's brilliant how simple—yet important—Anthony's message is.

You know when you see something that changes life for the better, maybe a new household invention or something, and you say: "Man, I wish I would've thought of that!"?

Well, when I read Anthony's book I found myself thinking the same thing.

But more importantly, I was also thinking: "Oh, yeah! I am *definitely* using this with my athletes."

This book couldn't come at a more opportune time, especially because of all the travel basketball being played. So many steps in a player's development are being missed and mistreated. And Anthony's always thinking of the player's perspective here.

When I look at a new product or resource I want to know certain details. For example, I want to know if it's results driven and not just a bunch of science that may or may not work in the real world.

But most importantly, I want to know if the information the

resource offers will set athletes, parents, and coaches up for success. Does it work in a positive way?

I can say without a doubt that the information Anthony's put together in *Go Prove Something! A Basketball Players Guide To Legally Using PEDs* will help athletes make stronger decisions as they build their "house" for success. I highly recommend this book.

Good luck!

Lee Taft
Greenwood, Indiana
August 2015

My Own Use of PEDs

I finally decided to ***Go Prove Something*** **(GPS)** to myself. The book you hold in your hands has been on the bookshelf of my mind for several years. I've been waiting for the right time to bring this to the public.

Is now the right time?

NOPE.

It will never be the "right time" to do anything.

So here I go anyway.

When I first decided to write a book, I came up with so many reasons why I couldn't do it:

- I've never written a book before.
- I don't have a college degree.
- I don't have any credibility.

I also asked myself questions, like:

- Why would anyone ever read my book?
- What if what I write is terrible?
- What if people laugh at me?

These thoughts and questions ran through my mind on a daily basis, until one day I said:

"STOP! **That's it**! I *need* to get this information out to the public."

So I wrote this book.

Go Prove Something! A Basketball Player's Guide to Legally Using PEDs was primarily written for school-age kids, teens, and children of all ages who participate in this wonderful sport of basketball. It's a step-by-step guide showing how to build your life from the ground up.

My passion is helping our youth become not just better basketball players but, more importantly, better people.

At the same time, this book has something to say to older generations as well. If that's you, there's no reason for you to stop dreaming. As long as you have a reason to move forward, the final buzzer in the game of life has not sounded.

This book compares the process of building a house to that of building up your own mind, body, and basketball skills. You'll learn to lay your foundation (posture). You'll build your frame (precision) and work on the roof and siding (protection). You'll also get to something just as important: your interior design— namely what makes you tick and how to use your mind to become a better player.

Now I will not make any promises as to what **YOU** personally will get out of this book. Everyone will take something different from it, and this is most definitely a case of the more you put in, the more you get back.

I will, however, make one promise that relates to everyone who reads this book. I have put my heart and soul into every single word of it. If I were able to download my mind into yours, this book is what you would get. And my sincerest goal is that it does nothing less than transform your life for the better.

I implore you to begin this journey with your own GPS Mindset.

That's right: **G**o **P**rove **S**omething.

Follow your GPS mindset in all aspects of life. In your personal development. On the court. In the gym. In your home. And even though you won't learn this stuff in the classroom, you can certainly utilize it there, too.

It feels so *good* to Go Prove Something to yourself.

And in this day and age, the more advantages you have, the

better.

You're embarking on a journey to improve your mind, body, and basketball skills. I'm going to take you places you didn't realize you could go. I suggest you sit up, prepare yourself for life-changing knowledge and, above all, embrace the journey.

Go Prove Something! A Basketball Player's Guide to Legally Using PEDs is not for the procrastinator. It's not for the person who just wants to fit in.

This book is for the person who wants better for their life and for the lives of their loved ones.

It's for the person who knows they were put on this Earth to do more, be more, have more and give more.

So please allow me to take you on this once-in-a-lifetime journey. I predict that by the end of this book you'll have experienced a paradigm shift in knowing how to build your mind, body and basketball skills.

So put your feet firmly on the floor and prepare to hit the ground running.

Take the time.

Read the book.

Internalize it.

Act on it.

You won't be disappointed.

Preface

Use **PEDs**. The End.

Thank you for purchasing this book.

Now: listen up.

As a basketball trainer for players of all ages, I'm making it mandatory that starting right now you use and become addicted to **PEDs**.

I can assure you with 100 percent certainty that all of the greatest players to ever play the game not only used but are still hard-core PED addicts.

Now, I know what you're thinking: "Has this guy lost his mind? Is he crazy? Did he really just tell me to become addicted to PEDs—Performance Enhancing Drugs?"

The answer to the first two questions is no. I haven't lost my mind. And, well, some people might think I'm crazy, but only in a good way.

The answer to that last question—did I really ask you to get addicted to PEDs?—is a little more complicated.

It's true that throughout this book I'll be encouraging you to use PEDs multiple times every single day of your life. What's more, I'll urge you to encourage your teammates, family members and friends to become hard-core users as well.

Let me explain why.

In my world, PEDs are not Performance Enhancing Drugs. My PEDs are more powerful than drugs. They're legal to use and cost nothing. If used consistently and at the proper dosage, the PEDs I'm talking about can take your performance to levels you never thought possible.

But I must warn you: these PEDs are *far* more addictive than their illegal counterparts.

How can this be?

Sit tight. We'll get to that. But first I'll give you an idea of what you're getting yourself into.

Let me start with what this book is *not*. Namely, it's not an exercise guide. I'm not going to spend time detailing the specific types of exercises you need to do to make yourself big and strong. I'm not laying out a program to make you faster. And I'm not going to fill your head with a plethora of drills to improve your basketball skills. I'm going to assume you've got a coach already, or a stack of books or list of videos to watch to work on all that.

What this book *will* do is teach you how to make PEDs part of your daily routine. I'll show you how to put them to use in basketball—and life—until they become second nature.

They'll enhance your game beyond what you may have thought possible.

Put what you learn in this book to use and you'll only be able to hide the fact you're using PEDs for a short period of time. Pretty soon you'll be exposed and everyone will know the truth: you're a hard-core user.

And just like with illegal drugs, some of your friends may join you and become hard-core users, but most will stay on the sidelines. In this case, applying peer pressure to those you love while sharing your new addiction will benefit everyone. This is peer pressure at its finest.

Using these PEDs on a daily basis will improve all aspects of your life. They'll lead you to:

- Take better actions
- Get better results
- Enjoy more exposure
- Reap greater success

Do I have your attention? I hope so.
We're about to dig deep into the world of:

Performance
Enhancing
Decisions

Hold on tight. Things are about to get intense.
It's time to change your life.
See you on the inside—if you think you can handle it!

1st *Quarter*

——— Chapter 1 ———

The Foundation (Posture)

A house must be built on solid foundations if it is to last. The same principle applies to man; otherwise he too will sink back into the soft ground and become swallowed up by the world of illusion.

~ Sai Baba

The foundation of a house is the starting point of construction. Your foundation has to be deep and strong enough to support everything that's placed on it. The deeper the foundation goes into the ground, the stronger and more stable your completed structure will be.

More often than not, laying the foundation takes the most time to complete. This is because once it's completed there's no going back. If errors were made or shortcuts taken along the way to save time, eventually they'll be exposed.

If you can truly conceive the amount of weight the foundation must support, you won't think twice about doing it perfectly. So as we embark on this journey to change your life, please: don't take any shortcuts.

Although you'll probably be tempted to skip a few pages or put off reading for some other fun activities, please do not. We are engaged in building a foundation for your life. Take this seriously. Make sure your own foundation is as deep and stable as possible.

It will literally make or break you.

The Foundation of Your Mind

Until now you've probably lived your life based on what happens to you and the circumstances you've been given. You have yet to realize that you have complete control over the thoughts that enter and remain in your mind.

Well that's about to change.

Throughout this book you'll learn how to control your thoughts by using different exercises designed to enhance your life in some way, shape or form. One thing I would like you to keep at the forefront of your mind going forward is this:

YOU can change all aspects of your life with one thought.

When building your mind from the ground up, you need to follow the same steps you would when building a house, starting with the foundation.

The foundation of the mind starts with that old reliable basketball term "triple threat."

In basketball, the triple threat puts you in the best position to succeed. It also provides you with the most options. When you're in the triple threat position you can either shoot, pass or dribble. Your *mental* triple threat consists of three things:

- An unapologetic belief in yourself.
- The gratitude to appreciate what you already have.
- A burning desire to achieve success.

Let's look at each of these in turn.

Belief in Yourself

Here's a quick question for you: what is thinking?

My take on it is that thinking is just asking and answering questions in your own mind. That's what you do all day long. It's that simple.

So I'd like to pose another question as we begin this journey:

If you don't believe in yourself, why would anyone else?

Think about that for a moment.

People won't believe in you if you don't believe in yourself first.

Understand that your mind works like a magnet. Have you ever tried to connect the negative and positive sides of a magnet? What happens? The sides are instantly drawn to each other, and once they get close enough they snap together. This is where the phrase "opposites attract" comes from.

Now, once you have one magnet connected, it becomes easier to draw other magnets to it. The magnetic force is stronger. So if you bring more positive sides toward the connected magnets the pull becomes stronger. And once connected the overall strength increases again. The more magnets that come together, the stronger the connection.

On the flip side, if you put the two positive sides or the two negative sides of the magnets near one other they instantly repel each other. No matter what you do, they won't connect.

Now let's mix this up a bit to show how your mind works. It's similar to the principle at work with the magnets, but in the case of your mind the attraction is positive/positive and negative/negative. That is, when you're in a positive state of mind you *attract more positive thoughts.* And the reverse is true: when you're in a negative state of mind, you get more negative thoughts.

As you've seen, it's impossible for two positive sides of a magnet to connect, and the same goes for two negative sides. But in your mind positive attracts positive and negative attracts negative. And what usually happens when a negative thought tries to work its way into a positively-charged mind? You guessed it: it's repulsed. Same with when a positive thought tries to take hold in a negatively-focused mind.

What you can do, then, is *take charge* and keep your mind focused on the positive.

Now, because of the way your mind works, belief can be your greatest asset or your ultimate liability. The old computer-related phrase "garbage in, garbage out" applies perfectly to your belief system. Since your brain doesn't know the difference between imagination and actual reality—that is, between your beliefs and what's happening outside you—you have an advantage in the way you use your mind (more on all this later).

Any successful person will tell you that all their goals and dreams started in their mind first. They went out and lived their lives based on what they believed about themselves. As Gandhi once said, "To believe in something, and not to live it, is dishonest." So *choose* to believe in yourself and have the audacity to follow through.

Gratitude

The next part of your mental foundation is gratitude.

Until you are grateful for what you already have, you will never be able to get to the next level in any area of your life. Being grateful is very difficult and can put your faith to the test, especially when it feels like everything's going wrong and you're not sure what's going to happen next. Nonetheless, always at least *attempt* to be grateful for what you have, and truly mean it. If necessary, make a list of things you're thankful for, even the little things.

Did you score well on a test?

Did you make a few extra shots?

Did you have fun with a good friend?

The universe knows if you're faking it. But if you continue to be grateful, even in the face of adversity and stupidity, the universe will conspire to make sure you get more of what you want and less of what you don't want. It really does work that way. I don't know why, but I *do* know you just have to have faith.

So try it! What's the worst that can happen?

The Burning Desire to Succeed

The last part of your mental foundation is a burning desire to achieve your definition of success.

Now I know many people might disagree with me and say that a burning desire should be the starting point of building the mind. But the way I see it, if you don't believe in yourself *first*, and you're not grateful for what you currently have, how can you have a burning desire for more? You might simply *want* more, but not be motivated enough to grab it.

Belief in yourself and gratitude inspire you to really want more—and they give you the *oomph* to go for it.

Desire comes from within. It's different for everyone, and comes in all shapes and sizes. For me, my desire to change the world comes from wanting to leave a legacy when I'm gone, while at the same time making my wife and son proud. I want them to know that I'm doing all I can to make our lives better. I want my son to look at me as his role model, as opposed to viewing celebrities, athletes or entertainers that way.

Either you change the world or the world changes you.

I'd prefer to change the world.

You need to dig down deep to find the desire inside that will keep you pushing every day. It's not easy. It will take a lot of questioning and answering in your own mind. And **NO ONE** can do that for you. You're on your own.

Then again, I hope you'll use this book to help you find your way.

The Mental Recap

So believe you can do anything you set your mind to. Be grateful for what you already have and what you've already accomplished. And do some soul searching to find out what your true desire for greatness is. These actions in and of themselves will change your life.

But this is just the absolute tip of the iceberg.

The Foundation of Your Body

Let's look at building the foundation of your body.

This'll be fun.

When you begin building the foundation of the physical body, the first things that should come to mind are the core muscles. These are the muscles of the torso, located underneath the coveted six pack. They act as a girdle, so to speak. Core muscles keep everything tight and do not allow your body to go places it's not supposed to go. In order to develop your core, you need to have patience.

The exercises you need to do are not quick. They are not flashy. They are not performed on the latest piece of exercise equipment designed to get you a six-pack in thirty days.

In fact, they're boring. They take time and require little to no movement in most cases.

Like I said up top, this isn't an exercise book—for specifics, talk to your coach or trainer—but I'll give you an example so you have an idea of what I'm talking about.

One of the best exercises that develops your core is the "plank." To perform a plank, get in the push-up position, lower yourself onto your elbows, suck in your gut, keep your back straight, and hold this position for as long as possible. Like I say, it's boring, but the end result is balance and stability (the true foundation) when you need it most. A strong core allows your cuts to be quicker and your movements to be more fluid, and it reduces your risk of injury.

The difference between athletes who possess superior stability and those who lack it is clearly visible, even to the untrained eye. One athlete makes crisp moves while the other makes sloppy ones. One jumps a little bit higher while the other stays grounded. One athlete is a little bit quicker while the other athlete always seems a step behind. One "takes a charge" while the other is called for a reach-in foul.

I think you get the idea.

The more stable and balanced you are, the better you will be. Period.

I'll mention one other way to help stabilize your body: developing proper posture. In order to do this, you have to make sure your major joints (also known as the "Kinetic Chain") are aligned properly during all your movements. Most players are not that far off in their natural movement patterns and just need minor adjustments. It's these minor adjustments that make the difference.

TIME OUT

Proper posture is:

- toes pointing straight ahead,
- ankles and knees slightly bent,
- hips back as if you're sitting in a chair,
- sucking in your gut, attempting to pull your belly button to your spine, and
- shoulders back, chest out and neck neutral.

Here are a few questions to ask yourself about your stability.

- Can you lift one foot off the ground and reach in all directions without losing your balance?
- Can you balance and support your weight during a one-legged squat?
- Can you perform a broad jump and land properly while keeping your balance and your proper posture?

Keep in mind that your body will always attempt to do what you ask of it. If you're attempting to make a back door cut to elude your defender and the muscles that you normally need to do this are not stable enough to support such a quick movement, your body will compensate and recruit other muscles to do the job.

Sounds great right?

In theory, yes. But for actual movement patterns that reduce the risk of injury, it's not so good.

When you stabilize your muscles during movement, your body will perform the movements it is being asked to do with the least amount of stress on the joints. If your body is *not* stabilized and you attempt that same back door cut, you have a recipe for injury.

Why?

Because once your body recruits the improper muscle groups in an attempt to complete the movement you're asking it to do, the primary function of that movement pattern has been compromised. Not only will you complete the movement pattern less effectively than if you had engaged the proper muscle group, you will also be asking *other* muscles to do something they're not designed to do. So a chain reaction begins.

Do you see where I'm going with this? Once you compromise one movement pattern, the next one is sure to follow, just as night follows day.

While this kind of problem might not initially affect you, over time the compound effect on your muscles and joints can literally be career ending. When you reach this point you're an injury waiting to happen.

Sorry to be so gloomy, but you need to understand the importance of what I'm saying here.

Bottom line: learn to stabilize and balance your body by engaging your core in every movement you make, and learn to move with proper posture.

Your foundation depends on it.

The Foundation of Your Skills

The foundation of your basketball skills consists of two things:

1. Understanding the fundamentals of the game, and
2. Your desire to compete in every single play.

The Fundamentals of the Game

Now, the phrase "fundamentals of basketball" means different things to different people. But in my world, the three major fundamentals of basketball are ball handling, layups and defensive posture.

Ball handling needs to be taught to every single player who steps on a basketball court. It doesn't matter if you're 5'2" or 7'2", if you are the superstar or the 12th man. You need to be able to handle the ball and protect it. If you can do this, your value to your team increases tenfold.

While there are hundreds of drills you can do that use two and three basketballs at a time, please start with the basics.

One basketball, two hands.

Get your basic crossover down pat. Dominate with a hesitation dribble. Go behind your back on the run. Stop looking at the ball when dribbling. Last time I checked, the game was played with one ball at a time. Master the basics and then move on to more advanced drills.

The next fundamental vital to your success on the court is the boring old *layup*—a two-point shot you attempt from below the basket by reaching up with one hand and bouncing the ball off the backboard and into the basket. A layup is the one offensive move that EVERY player needs to have in their arsenal. At some point during a game you'll be in a position to take a layup. Will you make it?

You'd better.

On a basketball court, there's nothing worse than missing a wide open layup. You can ask your coach how important it is because if you miss one you'll be sitting next to him.

Now I know you might be thinking: Layups? We're talking about layups? I got this. Next subject please.

SLOW DOWN there, Charlie.

Are layups easy? Compared to three pointers and dunking, absolutely.

And they're simple.

But in basketball and life it's often mastering the simple things that makes the biggest difference.

The magic is in the simple things. Most people don't master the easy things because they can get boring, and these people want *exciting*.

Get over it.

When players reach the point of feeling comfortable with their progress, they tend to move on to the next skill. I recommend that you don't stop at "feeling comfortable" and instead *master* the fundamentals.

If you can't be counted on to make a wide open layup, how will your coach trust you to make a jump shot?

That's easy: they won't. You'll be riding the pine, as they say in the basketball world. So make layups, plain and simple.

Now for the best kept fundamental secret you've never heard of: ***defensive posture.*** In my opinion this is a crucial fundamental that more or less gets overlooked. Honestly, have you ever heard of defensive posture as a fundamental?

I'll go with "no." Maybe that's why defense is considered an endangered species in the world of basketball today. Seriously though, this goes back to the fundamentals of the body.

Being stable allows your body to function with the least amount of stress on your joints. With less stress on your joints, your body can move more efficiently in any direction it needs to go. If you can respond to the offensive player's moves without losing your speed, balance or coordination, don't you think you'll have the advantage regardless of what *they* do? Makes sense, right? Most players don't take the time to learn how to play defense with proper posture.

My suggestion: learn it.

The Desire to Compete

As far as your desire to compete, I largely covered this in the previous section, *The Burning Desire to Succeed.* But since it's so important, here's a quick reinforcement.

Look deep inside yourself and find that desire to compete in every single play.

Here's an idea: *do what everyone else doesn't want to do, and do it to the best of your ability.* You'll already have an advantage. Make it a mission to master the mundane. While it's not easy to do it, in the long run it's well worth it. It will do wonders for your progress. While everyone else is complaining about doing the things that "need" to be done, you'll be making progress in the direction you need to go because you *are* doing them.

But you are the only one that can make that choice. Do it.

If you practice your ball handling, make layups, play defense with proper posture, and compete on every play you will be leaps and bounds ahead of your competition. While your opponents on the court—and on the playing field of life—are trying to make the highlight reel, you will be developing all the components required to create an unbreakable foundation in all aspects of your life.

Summary

The foundation is the most important part of any structure, whether it's a house or the mind, body or basketball skills. When you grasp the concept of how important laying a deep, stable foundation is—and then *do* it—you will be setting yourself up for success in whatever endeavor you choose to attack in life.

<u>*REMEMBER THIS*</u>

You can practice shooting eight hours a day, but if your technique is wrong, then all you become is very good at shooting the wrong way. Get the fundamentals down and the level of everything you do will rise.

~ **Michael Jordan**

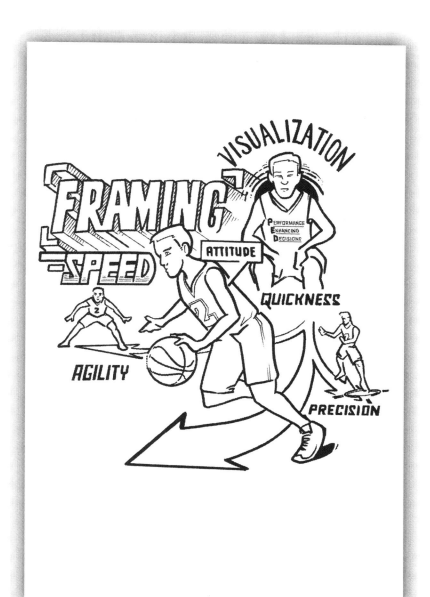

——— Chapter 2 ———

Framing (Precision)

Much as our skeleton serves as a structure for our bodies, the frame of a house is the underlying structure of the house.

~ Unknown

Framing—building the skeleton of your structure—must be as precise as possible. There is little to no room for error.

For example, when constructing a house, the spaces between the studs need to be accurate and well-placed. You have to use the right materials. The angles of your cuts have to be precise so they can support the weight you place on them. The posts that hold up the roof have to be evenly spaced—if you bunch three of them on one side and one on the other, you won't have a roof over your head for long.

The framing should take almost as much time to complete as the foundation. In some cases, even *more* time.

This same thinking applies to the nuts and bolts of framing your mind, body and basketball skills. Most people want to *go* through the day—not *grow* through it. Precise angles and balance are generally not high on their list during training. Don't let that be you.

Choose growth.

Precise growth.

The carpenter's expression, "measure twice, cut once," is a perfect model to follow. By approaching your own framing process this way you'll be more efficient with your time. You won't expend energy unnecessarily, and you won't risk injury by doing exercises incorrectly. Basically, you will not make as many mistakes.

Notice I did not say you won't make *any* mistakes.

You *will* make mistakes—as we all do. And when you do, correct them to the best of your ability and move on. Do not linger on them; doing so will negatively affect your future work. But learning from them and moving on can only help you.

This is true not only for the framing techniques we'll talk about in this chapter, but everywhere in your life.

Framing Your Mind

The three most important aspects of framing your mind are:

- the PEDs that you use EVERY SINGLE DAY,
- the attitude you choose on a daily basis, and
- your vision and visualization habits.

Now, there's that word again: PEDs.

Quick question for you, and be honest: did you read the *Preface* to this book?

It's okay. Lots of people skip prefaces and just dive in. But in this book, the *Preface* is important. So if you didn't read, it, go back to the beginning and check it out right now. It's short, but it's key to everything that follows.

So go ahead and read it. I'll wait for you.

. . .

Back so soon?

Great. Now do I have your attention?

Because this is one of the most important points in this book:

Use PEDs EVERY SINGLE DAY!
Become a HARD-CORE ADDICT!

Since you read the *Preface* you'll know what I mean. PEDs are not performance enhancing drugs.

They're **Performance Enhancing Decisions.**

And if you use them every day they'll take your game—and your *life*—to the next level.

These are the true PEDs, the only ones that matter.

And the first and most important PED you can make RIGHT NOW is to decide to use PEDs every day of your life.

Remember in the first chapter I told you that your life can change with one thought? Well, there it is. Use PEDs every day and watch how quickly that process can take place. Embrace it.

Performance Enhancing Decisions

Every day, on average, we make in excess of 35,000 decisions.[1] This includes simple decisions like when to brush your teeth, what shirt and shoes to wear, what to pack for lunch, what color pen to use, where you stand on the subway, and so on and on and on.

These aren't the kinds of decisions I'm talking about when referring to PEDs. But you probably knew that already. Although simple decisions like these can impact your life, they're generally just part of your daily routine and aren't particularly significant.

PEDs are decisions that *matter.*

Now, if you're expecting a big secret about what constitutes a life-altering decision, I'll tell you up front: there's no secret. I don't have some groundbreaking technique to help you make better decisions. Why not?

Because I honestly believe you already know what to do. For example, let's say you have a final exam tomorrow and you have not been putting in the necessary study-time. With the pressure on, there are a few things you can do. You can:

---

[1] See, for example:
http://go.roberts.edu/leadingedge/the-great-choices-of-strategic-leaders

- decide it's a lost cause and not study,
- panic and not study,
- beat yourself up about being behind and not study, or
- decide to buckle down and study your butt off.

Hmm… Which one is the PED?

Another example: On the court, let's say today is Monday and you have a game this weekend against your division rival. First place is on the line and you've been in a shooting slump recently. The decision you need to make is: do you use your free time to goof off with your friends or do you get your butt to the gym to work with your coach, figure out why you haven't been shooting well—and then train, train, TRAIN?

You can see that using PEDs is pretty simple. And although I probably don't need to make this next point, I will anyway: Using PEDs regularly doesn't mean you never goof off with your friends. That's part of life too, and a great part at that.

Sometimes, though—particularly when something big is on the line—your prescription calls for PEDs.

Let's consider something longer term, something we've already talked about. Remember in Chapter One we went over the importance of core exercises for your basketball skills? We said there's really nothing *fun* about these exercises, and you can certainly get by without doing them for a while. You may have good natural strength and agility. Maybe it's easier for you than the next guy to run and jump without tiring or risking injury.

But once you realize what core exercises can do for your game long term, what will you do?

If you're using your PEDs regularly, you'll do the core exercises. You may not have a smile on your face about it, but you'll do them.

Life is full of decisions like this, the kind with obvious consequences—whether immediate or further down the road. PEDs aren't just important in basketball and school. They can transform your relationships, your career options, where you live and even *how long* you live.

Basically, PEDs can change *everything*.

You Are in Control

Do you see how there's really no big secret here? How making PEDs is really not as difficult as you might think? I want to tell you something you already know, but may not think about much:

You are in 100 percent control of the decisions you make.

That's right. One-hundred percent. YOU decide whether or not to study. YOU either go to the gym and train or plop down in front of the latest social media site. YOU choose to get up an hour early to study or sleep in because you stayed up late watching TV. And so on.

This isn't rocket science.

Honestly, when was the last time that you really didn't know what your best decision was? If you're like me—like most of us, I bet—you usually know what you should do but, often enough, you just don't do it.

I should go to the gym. I should study for my test. I should take a hundred more shots before I leave the gym. As Tony Robbins so eloquently put it, we are "shoulding" all over ourselves.

Of course, guilting ourselves with "shoulds" isn't the way forward, but why do we so often do it? The "should" won't be necessary when we use PEDs to determine our next, best step.

We usually use "shoulds" when we're about to make an *excuse*. Think about it. More often than not we make excuses for why we *can't* do something as opposed to finding reasons why we *can*. We become what I call "excusologists." In fact, we can get so efficient at making excuses that we can easily convince ourselves that the right thing to do is too hard.

- I'm too tired to go to the gym.
- It's too hard to improve my footwork.
- I don't have enough time to finish that paper.

Once you decide to use PEDs on a daily basis, the desire to make excuses will gradually fade away. Your decisions become your guide—not your excuses.

We live in an era of instant gratification. We want instant results—or should I say instant *pleasure*? We don't worry about long term consequences. We don't think about what will happen days, months or even years from now as a result of a bad decision. We just want to feel good NOW.

I'm guilty of this as well, so I'm not pointing fingers.

The truth is this:

It's easy to break this pattern.

And an absolute *must* if you want to change your life.

All you need to do to break this excuse-making pattern is make a performing enhancing decision.

Let me give you another simple yet powerful example. Imagine that as a high school freshman you impressed the coaching staff and were selected by the head coach to become a member of the varsity basketball team. Here's your first PED-making moment of truth: do you get excited and party because you were selected? Or do you go straight to the gym and train your butt off to make sure you prove to the coach *and* yourself (GPS—Go Prove Something!) that he made the right decision?

See how easy this decision making process can be?

What "should" you do?

Which decision is "Performance Enhancing"?

Consider the following real-life example. On June 17, 1986, a college player named Len Bias was selected second overall in the NBA draft by the defending champion, the Boston Celtics. He was considered one of the best college players in the country. Needless to say, Celtic fans were ecstatic not only because they had just won the title, but because they had managed to draft such a promising player.

Everything changed two days later. On June 19, 1986, Bias made a decision that ended his life. To celebrate his new NBA life, he attended a party and decided to do something he'd never done before: cocaine. Not long after he had a seizure and was rendered unconscious. His heart and breathing stopped, and despite the efforts of EMTs and emergency room personnel, he was pronounced dead at 8:55 am.

Len Bias is known as the best player to never play in the NBA. This one decision of his proved fatal, and because of it the world will never know just how good he could have been, or how he could have impacted the game of basketball.[2]

Yes, I know: this is a worst-case scenario example. Most of your decisions are not going to literally be life and death ones, though some *will* be. But a decision doesn't have to be of the life-or-death kind to have consequences that may forever alter your career or health or life.

The Eternal Power of PEDs

Think of it like this.

If you throw a rock (your decision) into a pond (life) when the water is still, you'll see the splash it makes where it enters the water (initial impact). If you continue paying attention, you'll see what happens next to the rest of the pond (after-effect). The rock creates a ripple effect (a new set of conditions) in all directions.

The pond—your life—is never the same again.

Your decisions can change your life, and the lives of others, for good or bad.

Use your PEDs wisely.

---

[2] https://en.wikipedia.org/wiki/Len_Bias

Choose Your Attitude

Have you ever woken up early in the morning and just stared at the ceiling, thinking, "Today is going to be horrible; I don't want to get out of bed"?

How about those times when everything that comes to mind is just pure negativity?

Why do we do that?

Do you have any idea how bad that is for our minds?

All of us, regardless of age, have attended a Pity Party at Club Negativity. Most of us have done it multiple times. What exactly do I mean by this?

Well, it's when we feel sorry for ourselves. When we beat ourselves up for what we did or didn't do. Maybe we let our anger direct our actions. Maybe we missed a chance because we didn't jump at it. The list could go on and on, and when the pity party is in progress, it does.

What's important to understand is that this kind of thinking has a compounding effect. Do you remember what we talked about in the previous chapter, about how negative thoughts attract more negative thoughts? That's what happens at a pity party.

It might start with a small negative thought. Maybe you woke up a little bit late, stubbed your toe on the way to the bathroom, found a stain on your favorite shirt. Now you need to find a new shirt to wear, and because you're running late you miss your train by less than ten seconds and are late to school or work. All of a sudden it feels like the day is stacked against you.

If you don't catch hold of this feeling quickly, it can snowball out of control. In no time you might leap from thinking you're having a bad day to thinking you've got a bad *life*!

Do you see how easily things get out of hand if you let them?

STOP that snowball effect in its tracks before the bad day becomes a bad week, a bad month, a bad year, a bad decade—and so on. Understand that you have the power to change anything in your life.

Including your attitude.

You might be thinking, "What am I supposed to do? It's not *my* fault if I wake up in a bad mood. Besides, if I miss my bus and get in trouble at work, of course my attitude's gonna be lousy! How else would I feel?"

I can tell you one thing for certain: thinking like this is a surefire way to guarantee your bad attitude hangs over you like a black cloud. But you have a choice, and you can change your attitude. Let's look at one of the ways to do this.

Vision & Visualization

It starts with the visualization of your vision.

Do you know about the power of visualization? My guess is you don't or you'd be using it on a daily basis to create the life you want.

If you ask any successful person how they made it to the top they'll tell you this: everything they've accomplished began in their mind. Think about it. The lights you turn on. The clothes you're wearing. The bed you sleep in. The car you drive. Michael Jordan's amazing skill set.

All of these came into being first as someone's inner vision and then, through the power of visualization techniques, took shape in the world. This goes for personal qualities—like Michael Jordan's skills—and for any sort of invention you see in the world around you, whether it's your cell phone, the remote you use to change channels or the wheels of your car. *Everything* starts with visualization.

Your mind thinks in images. Have you ever noticed that? No matter what you're thinking about, the mind sees pictures.

Don't believe me? Here's a quick example: think of the color blue. Got it?

Now, did you see the word "blue" spelled out in your mind or did you see the actual color blue?

Admit it. You saw the color, and not "B-L-U-E."

Try again: See yourself standing on a beach by the ocean. It's a sunny day, with a bright blue sky above. Watch the waves rolling in . . .

Do you see how quickly your mind creates these pictures for you?

This is the secret to changing your attitude.

Try this: when your "opportunity clock knocks" ("alarm clock beeps" sounds too negative), press the snooze button and give yourself five minutes, but don't fall back asleep. Instead, keep your eyes closed and visualize how you want the day to go. Feel the feelings. Smell the smells. Taste the tastes. Hear the sounds. Envision your day being spectacular.

Then jump out of bed, get the day started with positive vibes, and make your vision a reality. If your mood starts to dip during the day, don't worry, just gently remind yourself of that positive visualization.

The Power of Visualization

You may have heard of a study conducted many years ago, in which a researcher studied players who practiced shooting free throws and players who simply visualized making them instead of practicing; both groups of players saw improvement in their shots.[3]

The subject of using visualization along with physical practice to improve one's ability has become a popular topic. We won't explore it in detail here, but I encourage you to look into it for yourself.[4]

---

[3] Clark LV. Effect of mental practice on the development of a certain motor skill. Research Quarterly. 31: pp 560-69, 1960.

[4] See, for example, Taylor J. Sport imagery: athletes' most powerful tool. Psychology Today. Nov 6, 2012. Accessed Jan 17, 2016 at:

For our purposes, what you need to consider is that *it works in sports and in life.*

So start visualizing, on a daily basis, what you want to happen as opposed to what you *don't* want to happen. Do your best to keep it positive at all times. Once you've visualized what you want to occur, act on the opportunities that come your way. If you have a longer-term vision as well, do something daily to bring that vision to fruition.

The Problem with "Hope"

Here's the problem. When things go wrong and we're hit with challenges, many of us just sit back and hope things will work out. We hope for a little bit of luck. We hope to just get through the day without things getting worse.

I'm sure you've heard how powerful HOPE is.

Well I'm here to play devil's advocate. I'm here to tell you that hope doesn't allow your mind to create anything. Hope is a *passive* state. When you just sit around hoping, you're not doing anything to affect the outcome of your day.

People often confuse hope with faith, but they're actually two different things. You put your faith *in* something. So you can put it into hope, or you can put it into your own power to change your day.

My suggestion? Don't hope. Visualize and *act.*

Be ready to attack the day the second you open your eyes. Pay attention to the way you're perceiving things and change your attitude if you feel it slipping into the negative. These activities will go a long way towards developing the frame for your mind.

I have a motto you can use if you like:

https://www.psychologytoday.com/blog/the-power-prime/201211/sport-imagery
-athletes-most-powerful-mental-tool
Also see Morris T, Spittle M, Watt A. *Imagery in Sport.* Human Kinetics. 2005.
Humankinetics.com

Visualize, Act, Become.

Broken out this means:

1. Visualize what you want to happen.
2. Take action in the direction of progress.
3. Become who you envision yourself to be.

Now *this* is a process you can put your faith in.

Don't Fake It!

Now that you're out of bed and have started your day in a positive place, your attitude will naturally be in a good state as well. Visualization and attitude go hand in hand. Makes sense right? The more positive thoughts that enter and stay in your mind, the better your attitude will be. There's just one catch.

Sometimes you'll find you've got all these great thoughts in your mind but you still have a bad attitude. Why?

Because, whether you know it or not, you're faking it. You're thinking the thoughts but you're not internalizing them, not truly believing them. You're not really being positive and somehow, someway, the universe knows.

TIME OUT

Look out for something called the "crab in the barrel mentality." When you put a bunch of crabs in a barrel and one tries to climb out, the others instinctively grab it and pull it back in. People often do the same thing. They see you trying to get out and just as you take your first step away from the pack, they pull you back down. The better you do, the worse they look. **DO NOT** let them pull you back down. Climb out and stay out. (I allowed this to happen to me for years. That's why you're reading this book now instead of fifteen years ago!)

When this happens, don't worry. It happens to everyone, and it'll pass. What I said about failure earlier applies to visualization too. When the negative thoughts creep in, even though you're pumping the positive ones into your mind, cut yourself some slack. A positive mindset will take hold with practice, and beating yourself up when you slip is counterproductive.

Framing Your Body

When I talk about framing the body, I'm touching on some of my main passions in life:

- Speed
- Agility
- Quickness

It's called "SAQ training." Once you've created proper posture and your core has been developed to withstand the rigors of being an athlete (see Chapter One), you need to move your body as efficiently and precisely as humanly possible. That's where SAQ training comes into play.

Included within the SAQ training is proper form. This should go without saying. All exercises need to follow proper form. If you do not follow this principle, you'll never reach your full potential and you'll set yourself up for injury. A simple rule to remember is this: quality over quantity. Never sacrifice form for more repetitions.

A lot of players, coaches and even trainers do not put the proper emphasis on SAQ training. They might run drills that they think are developing speed, agility and quickness. But everything has to start with the fundamentals we discussed in Chapter One.

If drills are not foundationally solid, they will lack effectiveness. Just because you're doing something doesn't mean you're doing it *right*.

Never simply equate activity for training.

Make sure you're doing the activity correctly.

SAQ Training

Here are a few simple definitions for speed, agility and quickness:

- *Speed* is going from point A to point B in the shortest amount of time possible.
- *Agility* is being able to change direction without losing balance, speed, power or coordination.
- *Quickness* is responding to external stimuli as quickly as possible.

When you combine SAQ training with proper form on all exercises it will set you apart from the average player.

Think about it: when playing basketball, you change direction pretty much every three steps. Because of that there's no need for two- and three-mile runs when training. But you *do* have to train at the same intensity and speed as a real game.

This is what set Michael Jordan apart from the other great players. Jordan always treated practice as if it were Game 7 of the NBA finals. He didn't practice; he *trained* (huge distinction). Jordan trained every aspect of his game until he couldn't detect any weaknesses. His teammates hated practicing with him because he trained so hard.

I challenge you to do the same. Be the player on your team that is hated for their intense practicing.

Training for SAQ requires the same precision as framing a house, which is why I cross reference the two. The angle at which you make your cuts when trying to get open or elude your defender needs to be precise. Spacing is key. The right amount of distance between you and your opponent can make the difference between getting off a shot or having your shot blocked. We are talking inches here.

What I mean when it comes to quickness is that, for example, you need to be a little bit quicker to get your hand up to deflect a pass your opponent is trying to make. You need to be a little bit faster than your opponent when going after that loose ball. You need to jump a little more quickly than your opponent when going for a rebound.

Basically, quickness means giving just a little bit more on every play. Is that too much to ask for on your journey to developing a total mind, body and skills transformation?

I think not.

If it seems like a tall order, remember that it's attainable if you follow a proven system. But it's *not* possible if you don't frame your body with SAQ training.

That said, I'll admit that SAQ training is also one of the most tiresome types of training to embark upon. It takes a long time and many repetitions to learn and master the movements. Pay attention to the details—those little details are often the hardest to understand and get right. That's the reason why most players don't put enough emphasis on them.

But if taken seriously, SAQ training can and will change your game. And don't forget: allow yourself to make mistakes—that's one of the best ways you learn!

Framing Your Skills

When it comes to framing your basketball skills, the component that first comes to my mind is defense. Defense can make or break you as a player. It is something that people do not take as seriously as they should.

If you can score the basketball or impact the game on the offensive end, you're considered a star.

But, if you can score the ball *and* play great defense, you're a *superstar* in the court of public opinion.

Ask any great coach and they'll tell you that defense is all about precise angles. (I say "great" coach because it takes the same attention to detail to become a great player as it does to become a great coach.) The better your angles are when attempting to cut off an offensive player, the better defender you'll be. By using precise angles and an awareness of the space between you, you can beat the offensive player to the spot they're trying to get to. This gives you yet another advantage.

Can you see how everything you do is integrated? Since proper body mechanics are always key to being a great defender, if you cut corners and are not precise with your angles, the results can be devastating, individually and to your team. If you slack off on SAQ training you might *almost* beat the offensive player to the ball—but since when has *almost* counted in basketball?

On the individual level, cutting corners in your defensive and SAQ training could mean less playing time, or even *no* playing time. From the team's standpoint, ignoring your training in these areas could cost you the game or even the season.

On the other hand, once you become an outstanding defensive *and* offensive player, you move into the realm of "superstar" potential. You become considered a complete player and not just a specialist.

Don't get me wrong, there's a place for you on any team if you're a specialist. But once you are considered a superstar, everyone from the coaches to the fans expects you to succeed more than you fail.

Don't fight it, embrace it.

Make defense a staple of your training. Many careers have been made on the defensive end of the court. Think Dennis Rodman, Bruce Bowen and Ben Wallace.

Will you be next?

Summary

Framing your mind, body, and skills is one of the most important parts of your life. Visualize what you want. Develop an attitude for success. Use your PEDs daily. Use proper form on all exercises and use precise movements during your SAQ training. Last but not least, play defense so you can elevate your game. Anything less would be cheating yourself.

REMEMBER THIS

But quality of work can be expected
only through personal satisfaction,
dedication and enjoyment. In our
profession, precision and perfection
are not a dispensable luxury, but
a simple necessity.

~ Niklaus Wirth

2nd Quarter

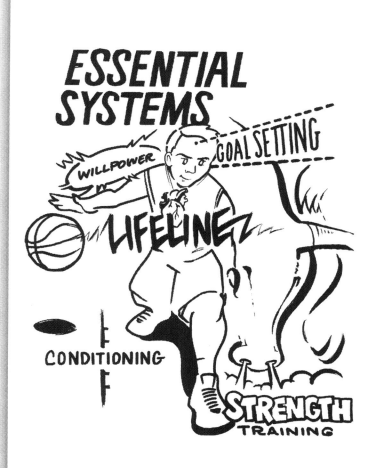

ESSENTIAL SYSTEMS

WILLPOWER

GOAL SETTING

LIFELINE

CONDITIONING

STRENGTH TRAINING

—— Chapter 3 ——

Essential Systems (Lifelines)

*We target people who understand that relationships are the
lifeline of a small business.*

~ David Rose

What's the first thing you do when you get home at night?

If you're like me, you turn on the light. If it's cold in the house,
you turn up the heat. If it's too hot you turn on the air conditioning.
If you're thirsty you turn on the tap and fill a glass of water.

And so on.

Heating, ventilation, air conditioning, plumbing and electrical
are some of the essential systems that make your house a home. If
your house has a great foundation and has been framed to
perfection but lacks these essential built-in systems, it's going to
be pretty uncomfortable—if not impossible—to live in. They're
the "lifelines" of your house. They keep energy, water, and air
moving throughout the space.

So once you've finished the frame you set up the vents and
ducts that distribute air throughout the house. You install the pipes
for the plumbing. You run the wires and cables that will make up
the electrical system.

You do all this and more to make the house livable, to make it
a *home*. Ideally, all of these systems will function synergistically,
without a hiccup. You turn on the light when you go into the
bathroom. You flush the toilet and don't need to look for a plunger.
You turn up the heat on a cold winter's night and turn out the light
before bed.

What's the alternative? The heating doesn't work and you have to search for blankets. The lights don't go on and you've got to remember where you put your flashlight. The toilet doesn't flush and . . . Well, you get the picture.

We tend to not think about these kinds of things unless something goes wrong. But if the essential systems of the house are laid out with care, there's far less chance that anything *will* go wrong.

So the question to ask is: why wait? When the essential systems in a house are working right, you can get on with the business of *living*. Why not be proactive and make sure they're installed correctly before you encounter problems?

As in house-building, so too with the essential systems of your mind, body and skills.

It's great that you've built a foundation and completed the framing of your mind, body, and basketball skills, but if you stop without developing your essential systems, you're basically running on empty. Then, when it comes time to follow through, you don't.

Most people get excited, start strong, make some progress and then—when things get tough or they hit a plateau—they fall back into their comfort zone.

Don't allow this to happen to you. You're better than that.

The trick is to get comfortable with being *un*comfortable, because that's usually a sign that you're making progress.

I'll share a secret: it's your *comfort zone* that's dangerous. If you stay in it too long, you'll never want to leave.

So don't get comfortable now; consider the comfort zone closed.

The essential systems we'll talk about in this chapter give you the *oomph*—and the requisite control over yourself—to keep you climbing to greater heights.

Essential Systems of Your Mind

At this point I hope you're feeling good.

You've taken some serious steps toward developing your mind. You believe in yourself, appreciate what you've already got, and have a desire for more. You visualize daily, have a positive attitude and are becoming a PED addict.

You do remember what PEDs are, right?

Good, just checking.

Now, installing the lifelines of your mind comes down to three essential mental systems:

- Setting standards
- Setting goals
- Instilling willpower

Setting Standards

Standards are the minimum acceptable benchmarks expected in a given area of your life. Standards are what separate the good from the great. The amount of effort you put into something is in direct proportion to the standard you set for it.

Think about this for a minute.

Let's say you're trying out and your standard is "I just want to make the team." Although this is your minimum standard, it's also your maximum. The effort you put forth is likely to be *just enough* to make the team.

This kind of standard is not going to get you to the next level, although it will probably help you make the team.

Now let's say you've set low standards for yourself but you occasionally do more than what's expected. For a time you may be considered an overachiever.

Great, right?

Well, yes and no. Most people only live up to their personal minimum standards. Even when they do occasionally overachieve, they eventually fall back to their minimum.

It doesn't *have* to be this way, but it often is. Why?

Think of it like a thermostat.

The purpose of your thermostat is to regulate the temperature in your house. If you set the heat to 73 degrees and the temperature falls below that, the furnace kicks on—and it stays on until the temperature reaches 73 degrees. At that point it shuts off. It doesn't come back on again until the temperature falls below 73 degrees—at which point the process kicks in again.

Now there's no such thing as an overachieving furnace that decides on its own to reach 75 degrees when its thermostat is set for 73.

But—and I don't think I'm reaching here—you are not a furnace.

You can set your own thermostat.

You can decide what your minimum standards will be.

You decide if you want to be just good enough to stay on the team, or whether to take your skills to the next level. You decide whether you're just going to pass a class or whether you'll absorb the material and reach for something more.

Your standards are what you'll settle for. And you'll find that when you set your standards high enough, limits disappear.

Goals

Without those limiting standards to stop you from soaring like an eagle, you can set your goals at any level you wish.

Goals are the second essential system in the lifeline of the mind. They are more specific, more targeted, than standards. A standard can be "I'll do my best," whereas a goal might be "I'll get an 'A' in that class."

Vince Lombardi, the famous American football coach, is quoted as saying, "Obstacles are what you see when you take your eyes off the goal." By this token, goals are what you need to focus on when everything else seems to be going wrong. They are the light at the end of the tunnel, the prize you keep your eyes on.

What are *your* goals? Can you see yourself obtaining them? If the answer is *yes,* you're starting to understand how the mind develops. If the answer is *no,* go back to the previous chapter. Remember the motto I suggested there?

Visualize, Act, Become.

The secret starts there.

And remember, too, that this is a process. You wouldn't expect to walk into a gym for the first time and bench press two hundred pounds. You'd work up to that.

So, too, do you work up to figuring out and setting your personal standards and goals. No one else can do this for you.

Success is like a staircase. You don't reach the top until you've climbed all the previous steps. The only time you start at the top is when you're digging a hole. Most of us having been digging at such a frantic pace that we don't realize just how far down we are.

STOP DIGGING and set your sights on your goals.

NOW!

Willpower

When you pull yourself toward what you *do* want, you simultaneously push yourself away from what you *don't* want. This is one of the most powerful aspects of goal setting, and it works in conjunction with the final key component of your mind's essential systems: willpower.

Something to keep in mind: it's very easy to set goals. Anyone can set a goal.

Achieving that goal is an entirely different color of paint.

When things get tough and you're tempted to sell yourself out and fall off the wagon, what keeps you moving?

Willpower.

Willpower is the ability to push away anything and everything negative that doesn't bring us closer to our goals. It's the ability to resist the urge to play a video game instead of studying. The power to eke out of yourself those last twenty-five free throws when you're already tired and just want to go home. Willpower is what makes you give that extra push during the game when it feels like you've already used up your reserves.

Willpower is like a muscle: use it or lose it. Like all the other skills discussed in this book, it can be developed. If at this time your willpower seems weak—you opt for the game more often than studying, you skip practice—don't worry.

Use your goals as an excuse to engage your willpower. Set your standards high enough so that your willpower gets a workout—kicking in more often than not, until it becomes second nature.

In time your willpower muscle will be one more tool in your kit on which you'll always be able to rely.

Yet at first as we pull ourselves towards our goals and push away from negativity, willpower is often a stumbling block. There's a simple reason for this:

It's easier to do the things you *want* to do than it is to do the things you *need* to do.

It's the pain versus pleasure principle. Most people will do what gives them instant gratification as opposed to what has long-term benefits. Because of this we're constantly in a "push and pull" state of mind.

I'm not going to tell you that if you just "think positive" negative thoughts will never arise. That's not going to happen. What I will tell you is that you have the ability to push those negative thoughts out of your mind just as quickly as they get in. It's not always easy. It'll take work. But if we've learned anything so far from this book it's this: whatever you do to change your life

TIME OUT

When you reach a crossroads where you have to decide to stay the course or follow the path of least resistance, a good question to ask yourself is this:

"Am I really *that* undisciplined?"

Think about it. Are you?

I hope not.

Because if you are, my work here is done. You might as well change your name to Mr. or Mrs. Mediocrity. Sorry if that seems blunt and borderline rude. But actually, the truth is that no matter what *you* think, *I* think you're up to the challenge. In fact, I think *everyone* is.

is going to take work.

Of course you'll make mistakes along the way. You'll falter, get upset, feel angry. It's okay. You're a human being. It's okay to have negative thoughts and emotions. Don't think you're a failure every time they get past your defenses. Just accept that you're having them—and then get them out of your mind as quickly as possible.

Now how do you feel about that question, "Am I really that undisciplined?"

Remember, life isn't about being perfect.

Remember, too, that if you don't like where you're at you can change it.

You know *my* answer already: *I* think that even if you feel undisciplined at the moment, you've got the power to change all that. But you also know by now that it doesn't matter what I think, or what anyone else thinks.

It only matters what *you* think.

Essential Systems of your Body

Your core is tight. You're stable and your posture is stellar. You move with precision and your form is to die for.

What else do you need?

Strength training.

The lifeline of the body is strength training. This is where all your hard work comes together and you start to become an athlete. Once you've learned to control your movements, building and strengthening your muscles to handle more tension and resistance drastically reduces your risk of injury and gives you a leg up on the competition.

You must train your body to handle whatever the game calls for. Whether you need to sprint, start, stop, jump, land, shuffle, pivot or change direction (the essential movements in basketball), your body needs to be able to adapt to the workload placed on it.

You accomplish this with consistent training sessions and a dedication most people aren't willing to surrender to.

Strength training is another area in life where you need to get out of your comfort zone. In fact, it provides a perfect metaphor for the whole idea of getting out of the comfort zone. If, for example, you keep lifting the same amount of weight all the time, you're never going to get past a given level.

This doesn't mean you have to lift the most weight or have the biggest muscles; it just means you have to push yourself past your personal best efforts. This is literally the only way to grow.

Athletes come in all shapes and sizes. No one is exactly the same, nor should they be. That's why there's no generic strength-training plan. Any plan you engage in has to be created for you and you alone. Talk to your coach, do some research, and figure out your best place to start—or to modify if you're already on your way—and go to it.

That said, every strength training program will consist of two constants: a pushing motion and a pulling motion. Most exercises that strengthen muscles and help them grow involve at least one of these motions.

To increase strength, resistance needs to be added to your exercises. This resistance can be increased in various ways. You can add to the number of reps. You can increase or decrease the weight. You can slow down or speed up the tempo of your movement. You can increase or decrease the rest period between sets.

Regardless of these variables, remember the cardinal rule of training:

Form always trumps the number of reps.

Quality over quantity is the rule to live by when it comes to strength training. In fact, it's really applicable in any facet of life.

Put another way: train smarter, not harder.

Essential Systems of Your Skills

You are now comfortable handling the ball. You're able to protect it from the defense. You're confident when called on to be the floor general, you can make a layup, and you have an unyielding desire to compete on every single play. You can stop on a dime, change direction with precision, and to top it off, your defense and defensive posture is turning the heads of people everywhere.

Now what brings it all together is the lifeline of your skills: conditioning.

Being in shape and being in *basketball* shape are two totally different things.

Basketball shape requires a plethora of movements that put a different level of strain on your body. Constant sprinting followed by slowing to change direction. Starting and stopping on a dime. Backpedaling as quickly as possible to beat your opponent to a spot on the floor. Jumping five times in a row to secure the rebound . . .

It all goes back to training for what your game demands. The reason to train at game speed is so you won't need to try and flip on the switch when the game is on the line. You won't have to ramp it up on game day; you'll already be ramped up.

Keep in mind when training: it's called a jump shot for a reason.

JUMP!

If you are doing sprints, SPRINT!

When you set a pick, hold it until the defender hits into you and then release.

It's really not complicated. If you're unable to push past the point of being tired in practice, how will you be able to do it in a game?

You won't.

Whatever you're doing, and whenever—during practice or in a game—do it to your best ability on every single rep.

Honestly, I find it unacceptable when a player falters in the clutch because they're tired. Whether it's not getting back on a fast break or failing to fight through a pick, in my opinion, being tired is no excuse. Training has to be a very intense process. Not only do you need to get into basketball shape—you need to *stay* in basketball shape. If you can jump high for the rebound one time, great. If you're tired immediately afterwards?

Not so great.

Conditioning ensures you can keep jumping just as high throughout the game.

Will Smith has a great quote to live by: "Stay ready so you don't have to get ready."

Summary

If I've done my job right, at this point you'll realize that you can have a strong foundation and precise framing, but if you don't master the essential systems of your game and your life, you'll get stuck in a holding pattern. Most people quit right before the magic happens. They get hit with some resistance and retreat into their comfort zone instead of plowing through adversity and making a difference in their lives and the lives of others.

Don't let that be you.

A little confession: When I ask someone how they're doing and their response is "same old, same old," it drives me up a wall. That should never be your response.

Commit to growing every day. Never let yesterday be better than today. If you can discipline yourself to stay committed to the steps that lead to success, the changes you see on and off the court will be amazing.

<u>*REMEMBER THIS*</u>

If you accomplish your goals too easily,
your goals weren't big enough
to begin with.

~ **Anthony M. Drago**

Chapter 4

Enclosure (Safety)

Your own mind is a sacred enclosure into which nothing harmful can enter except by your permission.

~ Arnold Bennett

Let's take a look at your house so far.

You've got a solid foundation in place.

The frame is standing tall.

The essential systems are set up; you can turn on the heat and the lights and flush the toilet, and you can count on everything working.

So what's next?

Look around. What do you see?

Wires, pipes, ventilation ducts . . . Not very pretty, is it?

Your house is primed for efficient living, but now it's time to enclose all those systems, to work on the interior and make it livable, fully functional, and nice to look at. This means laying down flooring, installing windows and doors, and setting up the walls and ceiling.

It means ensuring everything is safe, too. So you put covers on the electrical outlets and lighting fixtures. You secure the air conditioner in place. You attach the sink to the plumbing fixtures. And so on.

In other words, now you pay attention to some of the finer details.

Imagine having exposed outlets and wiring in your home. How safe would that be? Or imagine stuffing insulation into the walls but not covering it over with sheetrock and a coat of paint.

Sounds silly right? You'd never do that with a house.

But when it comes to your mind, body and basketball skills, this is exactly what most people do. They work on the big structural things like their foundation, but then neglect maintenance and the finer details.

Let's say you don't take the time to visualize one day. You fail to finish your last set of ladder drills. You don't make the two hundred shots you committed to but leave the gym instead after shot one hundred and seventy-five.

Get the idea?

You might be saving a little time initially, but in the long run it'll cost you.

So do things right the first time.

After all, if you don't have time to do it right the first time, when will you have time to correct it?

When you enclose your own interior you take all the skills you've developed so far and make them second nature. All that hard work you've been putting in is about to pay off.

Enclosing Your Mind

I expect that at this point you've made serious progress and are feeling pretty confident about using your mind to your advantage on and off the court.

Perfect.

But don't get cocky. You've only just begun.

Negativity has a nasty habit of showing up at the precise time you're feeling good. But if you learn to enclose your mind, all the work you've put in won't fall by the wayside. We do this through:

- Active thinking, which leads to
- Positive action

Thinking

I once heard a quote along the lines of "Thinking is hard; that's why most people don't engage in it."

It's all too easy to get lazy about thinking. We get used to ourselves, to our thoughts. We tend to think along the same lines, just like we tend to eat the same foods and go to the same places.

We *think* we are thinking, and of course in some sense we are. But what might come as a surprise is that we don't always know *how* to think.

Thinking is about creating. It's asking and answering questions internally. It's looking for opportunities as opposed to obstacles. We can use thinking to observe ourselves and see how far we've come, and how to move forward.

TIME OUT

"Rarely do we find men who willingly engage in hard, solid thinking. There is an almost universal quest for easy answers and half-baked solutions. Nothing pains some people more than having to think."

~ Martin Luther King, Jr.

Thinking can also involve spending time alone reading. When we take the time to listen to and learn from some of the greatest minds in the world, we can figure out ways to apply their teachings to our lives.

If you read a great book and come away with one idea that you can use to improve your life, it was well worth it. When we open our minds to the wisdom of others, we welcome in new ideas that can transform our lives.

Acting

A long time ago, I learned that every action you take is preceded by a thought. At first I didn't understand how this concept played a role in my life. Once I grasped it, though, a light came on—and my life changed for the better.

Let me show you what I mean.

In Chapter Two I explained that we think in images. So let's try an exercise here. Close your eyes and envision yourself standing at midcourt in Madison Square Garden. You're looking up into the stands and seeing thousands of fans.

Can you see that? (Tell the truth! Don't try to prove me wrong—actually try this out!)

Of course you can see it.

But the major question here is: *Why?*

Why can you see it?

You can see it because your mind creates a visual interpretation of your thought. The process is virtually instantaneous. But once you get the thought in your head (which you did when you read the above paragraphs), your mind helped you out by creating a picture for you.

Try it again. I'll make it even simpler for you: think of a basketball. Do you see the word "basketball" in your head or an actual basketball?

So what does this mean in the context of thinking and action? How can we apply this to the idea of enclosing our minds?

Let's head back to Chapter Two again for just a minute. You may remember we talked there about visualization, and in particular about a study of basketball players that showed that *visualizing* is a powerful tool for improving your game. These players used their thoughts to create images, and then took action—and their game improved.

Think of it this way: thinking leads to visualization and visualization leads to action. Your thoughts create images in your mind, and those images dictate the actions you take.

So if your thoughts are negative, your actions will be negative. If you think you'll never find a great job, you won't. If you think you won't make the team, you won't.

On the contrary, if you think you *will* find a great job, you will. If you think you *will* make the team, you will.

Now you probably see I'm being a little overly simplistic with these two examples about getting the job and making the team. I'm just trying to make the ideas clear. But the process doesn't always work out exactly according to the plan you think out in your mind.

More times than not, when one door closes another opens. You may not get *the* job you visualize, but when that one disappears another opportunity comes up.

The real problem is that most people spend all their time and energy focusing on the *closed* door (which may even have kept them safe in their comfort zone) and end up missing the newly opened one. Those who focus on the opportunity behind the new door tend to be the ones who take their lives to the next level— because they decide to open it.

In short, positive thought equals positive action. Think constructively, use positive imagery, and keep your mind enclosed, away from the craziness of negativity we live in today.

Enclosing Your Body

So how do we enclose this massive athletic body you've been developing?

Plyometrics.

You may not have heard of plyometrics before. Plyometrics are high-intensity exercises designed to develop explosive and powerful movements. The easiest way to understand plyometrics is to think of a rubber band. Imagine stretching it out and then releasing it. First you take it beyond where it is initially—making it taut—then you let go. The ends of the rubber band contract and rush back towards one another. As the remaining energy dissipates, the band resumes its natural, "at-rest" position.

When you do plyometric exercises, the same thing happens with your muscles. When you jump or make an explosive movement, your muscles stretch (loading phase), contract (explosion phase) and return to their original form as quickly as possible. How quickly your muscles can stretch and contract determines how quick, powerful and explosive you truly are. These are the basic principles of plyometrics.

However, most people don't want to learn the basics. They want to leap right into the fun and exciting exercises, like jumping and landing on high boxes and throwing tires around.

There are some fantastic advanced exercises that are honestly a lot of fun, but start with the basics and learn proper form.

Remember earlier, in Chapter Two, we learned about form in the context of SAQ training? Well, form is just as important here. If anything, plyometrics exercises are even more about form and less about the number of reps. It is *vital* that you use proper form when doing plyometrics in order to avoid injury.

Plyometrics in Action

So, I probably don't need to spell it out for you, but let's look briefly at how plyometrics can help you in a game.

Let's say you and your opponent are going for a rebound.

You both jump at the same time, and just as high.

The ball hits the top of the rim and bounces into the air.

You and the other player land at the same time.

Now because you've trained the way you have and enclosed your body with plyometrics, you should be able to jump *just a little bit* quicker to grab that rebound. Your muscles will react to the impact of your landing from your first jump and be able to *explode* into action again to get the rebound.

Dennis Rodman, one of the greatest rebounders of all time, once said that he was a great rebounder because he knew that no one else would jump five times for the same rebound. Most players would stop at four.

It's not about doing a *lot* more.

It's about doing a little bit more to gain that edge.

Plyometrics exercises complete the training portion of the body by enclosing everything you've created up to now. They provide power, explosion and safety as your muscles adapt to stretching and contracting at the rapid speeds you'll need them to in the middle of a game. In a sense, plyometrics training can help prevent your muscles from overextending or hyperextending.

That said, all the other elements of training we've talked about in previous chapters need to be in place in order to help your body handle the stress applied from plyometric training. Everything you've learned up to now needs to work in conjunction with plyometrics to transform you into a totally balanced, peak-performing athlete.

If you're not clear on the principles of plyometrics training, don't worry. I suggest rereading this section now while it's still fresh in your mind. Then talk to your coach or trainer, learn the basics, and get to it!

Enclosing Your Skills

Although it may not be considered an actual skill by most coaches and trainers, in my opinion *mental toughness* is one of the most essential skills you need to develop, and it can be taught, trained, and achieved like any other skill. Moreover, it should never be overlooked.

Why not?

Because it is what encloses all the other physical and mental skills you develop over the course of this or any other training program.

Mental toughness means different things to different people. To me, mental toughness means the ability to persevere through challenging circumstances. It reflects the ability to stay focused, disciplined and confident regardless of the outcome. In this respect, mental toughness can help in all aspects of your life, not just in basketball.

For some, mental toughness might mean being able to study into the wee hours of the night and pass their exam the next day with flying colors.

Another person might believe that a mentally strong player is one who demands the ball near the end of the game because they have confidence in their ability to score.

There's no right or wrong when it comes to what makes a mentally strong person. It's what it means to you. What's important is that you do not take it lightly. As with any skill, mental toughness takes intense training and discipline to develop. Even then, you will falter at times. It's been said that "success is going from one failure to the next without losing enthusiasm."

While this is true, I would like to tweak it just a little bit to be:

Success is going from one challenge to the next without losing confidence.

You will fail. Over and over again.

But so what?

I used to tout the saying, "Failure is not an option."

Now that I have matured (a little, anyway) and have had my share of life-changing experiences, I'm here to tell you something:

Failure is the ONLY option!

How can you know you've won if you've never lost?

How can you know you're happy if you've never been sad?

How can you appreciate success unless you've had failures?

You can't.

Embrace and prepare for failure (because it is coming), but don't lose your confidence.

Because failure is just a pit stop on the road to success. No matter how bad it seems, it's not that bad. When you find yourself in a tough spot that you need to get through, remember the old cliché, "this too shall pass," and press on.

Develop an iron clad mental toughness.

Summary

Enclosing your mind, body and skills is about focusing on the details and keeping up the momentum. It's about fine-tuning and embedding what you've learned so far. You've come a long way since starting on your own journey to GPS—Go Prove Something! Some congratulations are due.

But we're not done yet.

Our house isn't finished.

For one thing, we need a roof over our heads!

<u>*REMEMBER THIS*</u>

I've missed more than 9000 shots in my career. I have lost almost 300 games. 26 times I've been trusted to take the last shot and missed. I have failed over and over and over again in my life and **THAT IS WHY I SUCCEED**.

~ Michael Jordan

3rd *Quarter*

—— Chapter 5 ——

Roof & Siding (Protection)

On life's journey, faith is nourishment, virtuous deeds are a shelter, wisdom is the light by day and right mindfulness is the protection by night. If a man lives a pure life, nothing can destroy him.

~ Buddha

At this point you've completed the structure of your house. The framing looks beautiful, the interior is solid and fully functional and . . . well, what's next?

Look up!

For starters, you need a roof. And if you look around the outside of your house you'll realize there's another missing layer: the siding.

Both protect your house (and therefore you) from the storms that rage outside, whether rain, snow, sleet, wind—or some combination of all of them. They also keep the heat from escaping in winter; same with the AC in summer. The siding helps protect the frame from cracking or buckling when the temperature drops to -5° or soars to 100°.

And of course, both keep the bugs out.

The roof and siding are your protection from the elements. And why wouldn't you want to protect something you've invested so much time in creating?

As in house-building, so in life. You will always encounter elements beyond your control. This is why you can't skimp on *protection*. If you don't maintain your roof and siding, one good storm will wreak havoc on your interior.

Roof & Siding of Your Mind

You've come a long way in a short period of time.

You believe in yourself. You're grateful for what you have, yet you also have a desire for more. You visualize every morning, start the day with a great attitude and use your PEDs every day.

You remember what PEDs are, right? Just checking.

You've set lofty goals, raised your standards and developed the willpower necessary to navigate the storm of negativity by using your Go Prove Something! mindset. You're active in your thinking and language, and you take appropriate action in positive directions.

What more could you want?

There are two powerful attributes you can develop that will serve you well both on and off the court. The roof and siding of the mind are:

- Commitment, and
- Perseverance.

Commitment

Commitment is the guiding light of the mind. It's what enables you to follow through.

Most people don't take making a commitment seriously enough. Think about it for yourself. When was the last time you made a commitment to something and actually followed through?

Take a while to remember?

I can relate to that, to the kind of indecision that can lead to breaking our commitments.

That indecision needs to be replaced with PEDs.

NOW.

A commitment, whether we make it to ourselves or someone else, reflects the level of respect we have for ourselves. We're putting ourselves out there and saying, "I trust myself to do this."

And if we don't trust and respect ourselves enough to keep our own commitments, why would others commit to us? Why would they respect us if we don't respect ourselves?

Self-commitments are the easiest ones to make—and to break. After all, if there's no one watching over your shoulder except yourself, who but you will know if you break a commitment to yourself?

Luckily, I have a simple remedy for this:

Always do what you say you're going to do.

Commit to *commit*.

Think about what it means to really commit to something, and then *don't* commit to anything you don't fully expect to follow through on. That way, when you *do* commit, you take it seriously. You commit yourself to a goal and you don't stop until you achieve it.

Period.

It's really that simple. (I may have mentioned that I'm not introducing any groundbreaking techniques here.)

So why do commitments so often fail?

Because we know what we're supposed to do but we just don't do it.

That all stops now.

Like NIKE says, "Just Do It."

TIME OUT

"Commitment is doing what you said you were going to do long after the state of mind you said it in has left you."

~ Anthony M. Drago

If you're like most people, when you begin something new, you're probably all excited about the possibilities and the end results, so you set lofty goals and make some serious "commitments."

Here's a perfect example: generally there's a spike in gym memberships in the month of January. Some health clubs report an increase of between 30 and 40 percent.

Why?

Because people get excited about the possibilities. The coming of the new year makes them feel like they can turn the page on their old habits and start fresh.

But that initial enthusiasm wanes the further they get from January 1.

When the workouts start to get too hard or people feel like they aren't making enough progress—or get bored—they crash land back in their comfort zone and make excuses as to why they can't get to the gym.

This will never become you.

EVER.

Well, not if I have any say in it. And not if you have any say in it either. Commitment protects you from backsliding.

The good news is that you *can* have a fresh start. You don't even have to wait until January of next year.

Start fresh right now, this very moment.

Throughout this book I've been saying that *one thought* can change your life, so think of it this way:

A commitment starts with a thought.

A commitment *to* your commitment also starts with a thought.

All you have to do is start taking commitments seriously. Don't be making them willy-nilly. Make the ones that are important to you. And then keep them.

Perseverance

*Perseverance: A steady persistence in a course
of action, a purpose, a state, etc., especially in spite
of difficulties, obstacles, or discouragement.*[5]

So I've pointed out above that there's kind of an epidemic in the world today: people readily break their commitments. Whether it's to marriage or work or their team or to studies—whatever it is, many people don't *persevere* through the tough times.

The thing about tough times is that, ultimately, they're what build your character and lead to success.

I can pretty much guarantee that you won't realize how close you are to success while you're in the middle of the storm. At that moment it'll feel like there's no way out. And that's the moment most people will want to quit.

Let me give you a bit of advice:

DON'T.

Whatever you do, don't quit right before the magic happens. Trust me! Hold on just a little bit longer. It'll be worth the effort.

This is what perseverance means. Don't stop fighting for your dreams, NO MATTER WHAT HAPPENS.

You get that?

NO MATTER WHAT HAPPENS.

When there's no longer another option, the decision becomes quite easy.

Roof & Siding of Your Body

Your core is tight. Your balance is impeccable and your posture is second to none. You're moving with fluidity and precision on the court. You've developed some serious strength and great technique, and you're *explosive* when you need to be.

---

[5] Dictonary.com

Now what? You guessed it: protect it all.

How? Through training and maintenance.

The programs athletes use during the season are designed to keep them at the right level without pushing too hard. When you're engaged in this kind of training, something to keep in mind is that your progress will plateau. If you haven't put on muscle or gotten stronger and quicker during the off-season, it's not going to happen in-season.

Here's the kicker, though: no progress doesn't mean you're sitting idle, waiting for things to happen. Sometimes you need to work even harder just to keep what you've created.

The power of maintenance programs is that even though you won't see gains on them, you also will not see any drop off in power and fitness.

You might think this sounds easy. And it's true that building your body takes a lot more work than maintaining it. But it still takes hard work. You just get to linger in your comfort zone for a while.

Why?

Because you don't want to step on the court with exhausted and sore muscles from strength training. This will actually hinder the skills you've worked so hard to develop. It might also increase the chances of injury.

So protect them instead. Maintenance training will keep them where they need to be. It capitalizes on all your work leading up to the start of the season, without running the risk of setting you back at the very moment you need to give it all you've got.

If you're unsure of what your regimen for a maintenance program should be, it's best to ask a trainer. While some coaches do wear the hat of "trainer" as well as "coach," most are not qualified to do both.

There's a certain art to training that requires a different skillset from what you need for coaching. Some people can do both, but it's important that you get the right information. Everyone's training regimen will be different. You know how much you've trained preseason. The level of training you'll personally need in-season is going to be different from the next guy's. So don't take just anyone's advice, especially if it doesn't feel right. Make sure you get information designed specifically for you.

Seek it out, and don't stop until you find it.

Roof & Siding of Your Skills

You are now considered a *player*.

You've busted your butt and made some serious strides. You can handle the ball and protect it from your defender. You can consistently make layups and your defensive posture is excellent. You can run circles around your opponents because you've conditioned your body to do so.

And the best part?

You are so mentally strong that you rarely fail in a game because of a mental mistake. What once seemed difficult has now become second nature.

You should feel good about yourself.

Now it's time to protect the skills you've created.

So what's the "roof and siding" of your skills? Glad you asked. It's the infamous "blocked shot."

Now you might think I'm crazy for suggesting this. In fact, I can almost hear some of you guards out there thinking, "Why do I need to block shots? That's what the big guys are for."

I beg to differ.

Contrary to popular belief, the blocked shot is not only for the "big" guys, those players who can jump straight up and out of the gym. The blocked shot is something that all players should become proficient in.

Let's look at it this way.

Think of the advantage you'll have as a guard if the player you're defending not only needs to worry about you stealing the ball but *also* about you blocking their shot if they get past you.

(Of course, at this point they shouldn't be *able* to get past you, right? But that's another story.)

If they know you can block their shot, it'll be in the back of their minds, and for you, that's an advantage.

How does this protect all your other skills?

It forces the opponent to work harder on both ends of the floor, physically and mentally. They can't rest. What's more, if they're pushing themselves hard to keep up with you, that takes away from how hard they can push *against* you.

Just as *you* never take a play off, they can't afford to do so either.

But, the difference is that you've been training the *right* way for this very moment; odds are they haven't. Learn the blocked shot. Keep them on their toes.

Your versatility is your protection.

Summary

Protection is more about maintaining than it is about creation. Even getting proficient at the blocked shot is an important key to enhance the skills you've already developed. Mentally, it's about committing to the program you've already invested so much in, and persevering until you achieve your goals.

So you've reached the point where you can stand back and look at your handiwork and think: *almost done.*

That's right, *almost.*

It's time to step back inside, get down to the nitty-gritty, and design your life the way *you* want it to be.

REMEMBER THIS

The important thing in life is to have great aim and to possess the aptitude and the perseverance to attain it.

~ Johann Wolfgang von Goethe

——— Chapter 6 ———

Interior Design (Being Coachable)

Interior design is the ability to transform an ordinary space into a beautiful, well designed and functional environment.

~ Ann Snipes

You've got a house. Everything's working inside and out and there's a roof over your head.

Now let's make it a *home*.

If you look around your new place, you'll see it looks a little . . . plain. Not only could the walls use a coat of paint, but you might also be wondering basic things like: what will I sit on? Where's all the furniture? Not to mention the TV?

That's right. It's time for *interior design.*

Now, designing the interior of your house is an extremely personal thing. What one person thinks is perfect another might find boring. Some people like big open spaces and others like cozy setups to lounge in. One person might deck out their home in varying shades of green and brown, another might hate those colors.

It's all good.

What's important is that *you* like it. When your interior design is complete and matches the vision you have in your mind, you feel a sense of calm and comfort. Your place won't look like an apartment you're renting for a few weeks while you wait to move again.

In my case, when it comes to home interior decorating, I possess *none* of the necessary skills! It's safe to say I will not be hosting any of those interior design makeover shows in the near future.

So in my house, I hand the job off to my wife. She's the one with an eye for transforming a room into an *experience*. I do my part by contributing to the manual labor of painting and putting the furniture in place.

In other words, I know what my strengths and weakness are in this area, and I don't allow my EGO to tell me otherwise.

Some things I'm good at. Others I need help with.

This goes for all of us, in every facet of life.

Similarly, when you're designing the interior of your mind, body and skills, it's important to learn to be *coachable* enough to take direction when required. This is what allows you to get to the next level.

You start with a vision of where you want to be. You put your personal stamp on it, and you can take pride in creating it. But along the way you get the help you need to achieve it. Being willing to get expert help is one of the signs of a true leader.

Everyone has total control over how the interior of their mind is designed. So why don't they exercise that control? Because there's an epidemic of **ALMOST.**

Most people know what they need to do. They even know *how* to do it. But they don't make time to follow through.

So they *almost* make the team.

They *almost* lose the weight they want to lose.

They *almost* study enough to ace the test.

But that's not you, right?

I didn't think so.

So let's start designing.

Interior Design of Your Mind

The most important concept I need you to grasp from this

chapter is that you can absolutely, 100 percent of the time, control the interior design of your mind.

It's been said that 3 percent of the people control 97 percent of the wealth in this country, and that 97 percent of the people work for the top 3 percent.

That being said, if you were to ask one hundred people if they can control their minds, I believe that ninety-seven of them will tell you they can't (unless you happen to be in a room full of entrepreneurs and visionaries).

I'm here to tell you that those ninety-seven people would be *wrong*.

But you're probably not surprised to hear that from me. After everything we've learned up to this point, I think you might even agree with me.

Now I'm sure those ninety-seven people would *like* to control their minds, but they believe they don't know how. So let's teach them by example.

How do you control your mind?

You've already picked up some methods in this book, and committing to them is a great step to take. At the risk of sounding vain, I implore you to re-read this book several times. You'll probably pick up something new each and every time. I can say this because I've done the same with many other books.

Many years ago, I learned from world-famous success coach Tony Robbins that repetition is the mother of all learning.

If you've really been paying attention, you'll probably have noticed that I allowed for a lot of repetition in this book. I'm constantly repeating things so they get anchored in your mind and become second nature.

The more you *hear* something, the more likely it is to take root in your mind.

The more you *do* something, the more efficient and successful you'll become at it.

That's why it's imperative to begin with the fundamentals. If you're learning something new you need to make sure you're doing it correctly from the start. If you learn it the wrong way, you're going to have to *un*learn it before you can get it right.

That's how powerful repetition is.

And that's how it works for your mind, body and basketball skills, and everywhere else in life.

So reading this and other books again and again will help you really commit to—and USE—the advice contained within them.

There are so many amazing books and recordings that can be referenced to help you develop your mind. And by developing your mind, you're actually taking charge of it.

Way back in Chapter One, I used the phrase "garbage in, garbage out" when talking about beliefs. The same rule applies here: the more good stuff you put into your mind—in the form of great ideas from books and recordings and trusted people and so on—the more *great* stuff you'll get out of it.

This is how you design the interior of your mind: take in new information, see what works for you, and then commit to using it in your life. Commit to being coachable, to always learning and adapting. Stay focused on the task at hand. Give and get as much as you can from it.

Take control of your mind.

Let me share with you an example of how powerful the mind is. It's a little like the basketball study we talked about in Chapter Two, but it goes into a bit more depth.

Years ago, two researchers assigned thirty athletes into one of three groups. The first group would do mental exercises on their hip flexor muscles. The second would do actual physical exercises. The third would do neither. At the end of the study, the group doing mental exercises improved their physical strength by 24 percent. Those who did the physical exercises improved by 28 percent, and the group doing neither did not improve at all (perhaps no surprise there).[6]

Mind blowing right?

To put it another way: it's been scientifically proven that the mind cannot differentiate between real life and imagination. Your mind is extremely powerful and *it will do whatever you ask it to do.*

Interior Design of Your Body

You've worked your tail off to build the body of a totally balanced, peak-performing athlete. You've broken down more muscle fibers than you can possibly imagine. Now part of the design process is to take the necessary steps to let those muscles repair themselves. This takes time and patience, but it's vital.

Why?

If you don't allow your muscles to repair properly after working them hard, you'll create knots and tightness within them and set yourself up for injury. You won't be able to achieve optimal range of motion.

So how do we get our joints and muscles to work together and allow for a healthy range of motion?

STRETCHING.

Slow and controlled stretching (aka, "static stretching"). Thirty seconds or so for each stretch, each side of the body.

Always stretch evenly. By "evenly" I mean this: if you stretch the right side of your body, stretch the left side of your body. Never focus on only one side of the body. Without getting too technical, static stretching pushes your muscles past the point of resistance and the normal range of motion. By stretching and

---

[6] Shackell, Erin M.; Standing, Lionel G. Mind Over Matter: Mental Training Increases Physical Strength. April 2007. North American Journal of Psychology; 2007, Vol. 9 Issue 1, p. 189.

releasing in this fashion, you can help your muscles grow longer and increase your range of motion.

Optimal range of motion is the key to any athletic movement.

TIME OUT

"There can be danger in stretching your body if not done properly. The same is true with the imagination and the chemistry which may give the imagination elasticity, but the soul gives a direction."

~ Eugene J. Martin

Make it a "must" to stretch every day. You can do it after your training session, game, practice, or at night before bed. The key is to stretch daily so your body moves and reacts the way you want it to, when you want it to.

As with all the exercises we've discussed in this book so far, don't just jump in and try to touch your toes or do a full split! Take your time. Talk to your coach or trainer and read about the right way to stretch. If you don't do it *right* you're setting yourself up for injury.

And why do that when we're so close to the finish line?

Interior Design of Your Skills

Guess what?

You're now a bona fide basketball player. Congratulations. (I know I keep saying that, but at this point you deserve it.)

You've come a long way and developed a more diversified set of skills than most of the players you'll encounter on the court. You've clearly got an advantage.

So what else is there to work on?

Two things. Two skills that get overlooked by most trainers and coaches but which play a huge role in defining and shaping your game:

- Being coachable
- Being a great teammate

Being Coachable

We've talked above about being coachable in a couple of different contexts. And just as you want to keep your mind open and downloading information in the form of books and audios or whatever, so too do you want to listen to your coach or trainer.

Just like when you're building a house and don't know how to properly set up the frame or wire for electricity, you don't know everything about how to get in shape and play the game.

That's why we call in the experts.

Believe it or not, most coaches *do* know what they're talking about. Of course they can make mistakes—who can't?—but you need to put your trust in them over the long haul. You need to buy into their system and philosophy of coaching.

If you don't, you'll find yourself outside looking in for most of your games.

Most coaches have been in the game for a while. They know what works and what doesn't. They have insights garnered from long hours of watching players and plays, game after game after game. A lot of them have studied the greats. They think about the individual and they think about the team. And they can share this with you, if you're willing to listen.

Be coachable. Open up to the situation you're in and see what you can learn from it. If things keep going south, figure out what the problem is.

Sure, maybe every once in a long while it might be the coach or trainer.

But I'd lay odds that *you* can do more to improve whatever situation you find yourself in, and you'll be the better for it.

Rule of thumb for success?

Let your coach coach and your trainer train.

Be a Great Teammate

Believe in your teammates. This means more than just encouraging them. It's also about trying to help your team improve any way you can.

If you're having a bad game and the coach decides you're hurting the team more than helping it, he'll replace you.

If that happens, what's the first thing you should do?

Embrace it. That's step one of being a great teammate. But your job doesn't end there. You also need to genuinely support the player who replaced you. Doing so doesn't mean you've lost your drive to compete. It just means that you want nothing more than for your team to succeed by any means necessary.

Even if that means your taking a back seat. You do what needs to be done for the team.

Besides, odds are you'll get another opportunity to shine. Then, when that happens, maybe somebody on the bench will be cheering for *you*.

Summary

We're *so close* to the end!

Your house looks beautiful inside. You've taken great strides towards controlling your mind, taking care of your body, and supplementing your basketball skills with a love for your team and a willingness to be coached.

Feeling good about yourself?

You should be.

Is it time to celebrate?

Almost.

But first, let's step back outside . . .

REMEMBER THIS

Once the person commits to being coached, he/she begins to experience a different, more hopeful world as his or her perceptions change.

~ **John G. Agno**

4th Quarter
(CRUNCH TIME)

—— Chapter 7 ——

Exterior Design (Leadership)

You've got to be willing to do the things today that others won't do in order to have the things tomorrow that others won't have.

~ Les Brown

So you're standing outside admiring your handiwork. The house looks great. Nice roof and siding, of course, and the frame looks sturdy and strong. What more can you do?

Take a look around. You'll see leftover construction materials and barren ground instead of a lawn. There's no garden to speak of—yet—and the driveway is just a stretch of gravel leading from the road. Your property line might look nice bordered with some shrubs. And when you look more closely you can see a thin film of dust kicked up from the construction that's coating the windows of your new home.

It's time to take charge of the exterior design of your house.

Do some landscaping. Plant and prune those shrubs. Pave your driveway and power wash the siding and deck. Clean the windows. How your home looks on the outside is a direct indicator of how it looks on the inside. So make the exterior of your house reflect the investment you've already made on the interior.

As with interior design, what you choose to do with the exterior of your house—and your mind, body and skills—is largely a personal choice. But I am going to guess you'd prefer that it sets a positive example, that it be unique and reflect who you truly are.

At this point in their development, many people become satisfied with what they've accomplished and take their foot off the gas.

Don't do that.

The exterior design is the cherry on top of the sundae of life. That may sound corny, but it gets to the point. While this is definitely a time to celebrate and enjoy your success, you don't want to spend too much time patting yourself on the back.

The people who set themselves apart from the masses embrace their success, enjoy it—and then set the bar higher for their next goal. That is what *leadership* is all about: raising your standards and the standards of those closest to you. It's about setting an example, taking responsibility for things even when they're not your responsibility, and showing poise when everything seems to be going wrong.

Remember what I said above: the outside of your house is a direct reflection of what it looks like inside. This is true for your mind body and skills as well. We have reached the final step in creating the person you want to be—and the person everyone else sees.

So let's finish strong.

Let's learn to lead.

Exterior Design of Your Mind

When it comes to the exterior design of your mind, the finishing touches are:

- Personal growth, and
- Contribution to society.

These traits make you a leader in every sense of the word. As we grow older and reflect on our lives, we will look back and see how we've progressed and who we've helped along the way. That's just human nature.

Personal growth and our contributions to the world around us are a result of our putting into action all the things we've listened to, read and learned over the years (as we just discussed in the previous chapter). The traits are intimately connected. What amazes me to this day is that we grow as people when we help others. In fact, we *can't* grow without helping others, and we can't help others without growing.

It's actually a pretty awesome way to live your life, if you ask me.

Now, helping others doesn't necessarily mean giving them financial aid. More often than not, it doesn't have anything to do with that.

Most people are looking for feelings of appreciation and significance. They want to know that they matter and that they are on this Earth for a reason.

I heard a saying a long time ago that went something like "Appreciation: babies cry for it and adults will die for it."

Although they might not admit it, a lot of people would probably prefer sincere appreciation for the work they do rather than more money.

In order to grow, we need to constantly be doing things that others often don't want to do.

The mundane.

The repetitious.

The studying.

The training.

And so on.

So much effort goes into developing oneself that a lot of people simply won't make the time to do it. But when *you* do it, and when you then use your ever-expanding skills and knowledge to contribute to society, you become a true leader.

Ask yourself: What have you done to change the world?

I don't mean "What have you invented?" or "What movement have you started?" People are often under the impression that in order to change the world, you have to be famous. You have to influence a bunch of people or do something huge so everyone notices.

Not the case.

Try out this exercise. This week, help two people with whatever they need help with. It doesn't have to be related to sports. Just lend a helping hand where needed. Then ask them to pay it forward and help two other people in the same fashion.

Now that's *four* people that have been helped. Those four go out and each one of them helps two more people, and all of sudden eight people are being helped.

Let's play with the numbers a bit more. If you help one more person in addition to the first two, then you've helped three. If those three help another three and so on and so on, you go from three to nine to twenty-seven to eighty-one . . . and so on. All of these people being helped in some way with a wave that you started.

That's pretty awesome.

I believe that deep down we all want to help, to contribute to the world and leave our stamp on it. The problem is that most people don't know where to start. So here are a few examples.

- Help a neighbor carry his groceries into the house.
- Help a classmate understand something that comes easy to you when you see her struggling in a certain subject.
- Help an elderly person who has trouble opening the door to a restaurant.
- Volunteer at a local food bank.

This is a short list, but I think you can get the idea from it. The possibilities are endless.

Businessman and motivational speaker Zig Ziglar has a great quote:

**If you help enough people get what they want,
you will eventually get what you want.**

This, of course, shouldn't be your only reason for helping others. But it's certainly icing on the cake. The true joy comes in the helping. And it's nice to know, too, that your actions have made the world a little better for someone else.

TIME OUT

"Successful people are always looking for opportunities to help others. Unsuccessful people are always asking 'what's in it for me?'"

~ Brian Tracy

Exterior Design of Your Body

The exterior design of your body also comes down to two things. In keeping with the idea of leadership, we'll focus on taking charge of your planning and your contribution to others in the physical fitness arena.

Planning

Let's start with two relevant quotes:

Plan your work and work your plan.

If you fail to plan you plan to fail.

Planning will take some work. That's why it's under the heading of exterior design of your body. Can you develop a great body without planning your workouts, meals, sleep schedule and so on?

Well, yes, to a certain degree.

But it's not very likely you'll attain the heights of agility, strength, explosiveness and power—or that you'll be as *mentally* tough—if you try to just wing it.

The reason is that a proper plan ensures you get everything done, and get it done *right*. Let's face it: life is complicated. We've all got a lot going on, whether it's work or school or training or reading or whatever. And let's not forget all-important family time and just hanging out with your friends and relaxing. All of these things are vital for a happy, healthy life.

How do you ensure you fill your time with the right balance of them?

A plan.

That's one of the reasons I've laid this book out the way I have: to help you see how this stuff is all connected so you can incorporate it into your planning and take charge of your life.

A leader starts out by learning how to lead himself.

Planning takes the guesswork out of your daily routine. With a good plan in place you won't find yourself at the end of the day wondering how you missed your workout time or forgot to study for tomorrow's test. You won't realize you haven't eaten since breakfast and you're only going to get three hours of sleep because you forgot about that early morning training session.

You'll have ensured that none of this bad stuff will happen because you've planned ahead of time to make sure you get everything done.

Now don't think I'm saying you've got to plan everything down to the last minute. You can leave room for spontaneity, for the magic in life.

The irony is that when you plan you *open up* room for downtime and spontaneity. You don't have to worry about how you're going to fit everything in if you've already planned for it in advance.

So pull out a pen and paper or open an app and lay out the

schedule for your day. If you're new to the process, it'll take some experimentation to get a solid plan in place. Maybe start with putting the big things, the most important ones, down first. Then plan the other stuff around them.

It might seem like an extra effort at first, but pretty soon you'll see it gives you more control over your day—and even more free time by making you more efficient.

Contribution

When it comes to exterior design and your body, think in terms of helping others with their own physical fitness. Share what you know. Show people the proper way to do things—the proper form, the right way to do an exercise—if you spot them doing something wrong.

You don't do this in an arrogant way, but in a helping and humble one. Explain you used to do the same thing but learned the correct way. You can use something I learned about years ago from Steve Carter, one of my mentors. I still use it today.

It's called the "Feel, Felt, Found" method.

If you see someone frustrated and struggling with something, or simply doing it wrong, you can tell them:

"I understand how you FEEL. I FELT the same way. But I FOUND out the proper way to do that."

Simple, but it takes into account their feelings and it lets them know you're not trying to lord anything over them. Being humble in your approach will assist in lowering a lot of emotional walls. People will be able to relate to you. They'll know you're one of them.

This, incidentally, is also a good rule of thumb to keep in mind for leadership. Leading isn't about being better than other people. It's simply about helping them see the way forward.

So don't be afraid to help. And if you get rejected, oh well— it's their loss. Whether you realize it or not, most people do want help. They're just too scared or too embarrassed to ask.

So be a leader, and offer.

TIME OUT

"Our goals can only be reached through a vehicle of a plan, in which we must fervently believe, and upon which we must vigorously act. There is no other route to success."

~ Pablo Picasso

Exterior Design of Your Skills

In keeping with the theme of this chapter, we'll narrow our focus to developing two key skills to top off your own personal exterior design and training:

- Leadership, and
- Contribution.

Sound familiar? Are you seeing a pattern here?

I certainly hope so.

By now you're already a solid basketball player with loads of potential. But like I've been saying all along, there's always another level you can take it to.

Leadership & Contribution

These two are so intertwined here, there's no point in putting them in separate sections. It's simple really: your leadership is your contribution.

You give the best of yourself on and off the court; others follow your lead and everyone benefits.

Believe it or not, leadership is a rare commodity in the sports world. Not everybody can lead and, quite frankly, most don't want to. Leading a group is a huge responsibility and not for the faint of heart. I'm not just talking about leading on the court. You've got to lead *off* the court as well.

This exemplifies true leadership.

Now some of you may argue that leadership is not a skill. And even if you allow that it *is* a skill, you might not believe it can be taught.

Of course, I beg to differ.

Simply by having read thus far in this book, you're already on your way to becoming a leader.

In the basketball world, our leadership skills come as a result of being an extension of the coach, regardless of the role you play on the team. Part of it, as we talked about earlier, is buying into your coach's system and philosophy on a personal level but also, and more importantly, reinforcing it with all your teammates. Know your role and fulfill your role.

This is leading by example.

You can do this in other ways, too. By helping set the tone for practice and training sessions. By supporting those around you. By putting into effect what you've learned in this book and sharing it with others.

You don't need to be the "superstar" to be the leader.

You *do* need to be present and active and supportive.

My dad used to tell me, "Do as I say, not as I do."

I love my dad, but that never made sense to me.

As a leader, I cannot expect others to do what I am not prepared to do myself.

You want your team to train longer or put in extra work? You have to do it first.

You want to have good morale on your team? It starts with you.

Try this: *initiate* whatever you want to see more of from your team on the court and more often than not I'll bet you it'll begin to happen. People will see what's working for you and adopt it for themselves.

Does that mean you win every game and things always work out in your favor?

Abso-freakin-lutely not.

But your odds of success will improve drastically. Plus, you'll have the satisfaction of knowing you're being and giving your best.

Summary

That's it.

You've made it. Time to celebrate.

Am I serious this time? Yep.

Sure, I've got *one* last trick up my sleeve, and we'll get to that in the last chapter, but, really, now's the time to kick back and relax for a minute.

Embrace the journey.

Maybe you've been doing all the exercises in this book as you read along, or maybe you thought you'd read it first, and then begin. Either way is great.

But when you *do* fully engage with the work in this book and reach this point, you'll understand a few things about yourself. Namely:

- You can do things you probably never thought possible.
- You can push past the comfort zone that's been holding you back for far too long.
- You can grow in all facets of your life.
- You can pick up skills that are so advanced you'll barely recognize yourself after a while.

This isn't a matter of luck.
You've busted your butt like never before.
The result?
You're a totally balanced, peak-performing individual.
It's party time.
Enjoy.

<u>*REMEMBER THIS*</u>

Be the change you want
to see in the world.

~ Gandhi

HOLD ON A MINUTE!

PUT DOWN YOUR CELL PHONE.

CHECK YOUR EMAIL AND SOCIAL MEDIA LATER.

I've got one last question for you.

Since everything's going smoothly now, do you think it'll always stay that way?

I wish I could tell you "yes," but that's not even close to the truth.

I've waited until now to hit you with the hardest part of your mind, body and skills training. This'll make everything you've done up to this point seem like learning your ABCs and 123s.

Seriously? you ask me. Does this ever end?

Well, as with everything else, that totally depends on *you*.

Chapter 8

The Profender (Adversity)

How you respond to the challenge in the second half will determine what you become after the game, whether you are a winner or a loser.

~ Lou Holtz

Well, life is good.

Your house is amazing. Your mental toughness is ironclad. Your body is as close to perfection as possible and you're leading your team to the promised land.

Until . . .

You relax.

You get too comfortable.

And you take your foot off the gas.

Then what happens?

BAMMMMM!

It hits you like a ton of bricks. The air conditioning stops working. The toilet backs up. The tree you neglected to prune drops a branch on your roof. The siding buckles in the sun and the bugs get in.

In the language of your mind, body and skills, you strain a muscle while working out. You land wrong and twist your ankle. You miss an easy shot at a critical moment because you've been slacking off on practice.

That, my friends, is what we call *adversity*.

In every area of life, it's easy to fall off the tracks, especially when things are going good. That's when you can get complacent.

You've busted your butt, and maybe a part of you thinks you're entitled to smooth sailing from here on out.

Guess what? That's not how real life works. That's Hollywood. You will always be hit with adversity.

Let me repeat that.

You will *always* be hit with adversity, especially when you least expect it. So here's an idea:

EXPECT IT.

We can think positively and work to avoid crises, but life is complicated and adversity is part of it. So if you know it's coming at some point, you can prepare for adversity by training your mind, body and skills.

Sure, that's what you've been doing for this whole book (or at least I hope you've been doing it). But in this final chapter I want to share a few final tips to keep you on your toes.

Not so you're walking around always expecting the worst. That's no way to live. But so you *do* know what to do when adversity strikes.

Like I say: it will.

But now you'll be ready for it.

The Original Profender

But first let me give you a quick history lesson about the *actual* Profender, and tell you want it is.

The Original Profender was created in 2008 by my good friend and brother from another mother, Tony Devine. Tony was trying to figure out a way to help his son, Devon, practice his shots in a more realistic, game-type setting. He wanted something that would help him learn to jump and shoot higher and avoid getting his shots blocked.

After coming up empty-handed from hours of searching online, he realized what he needed was something *mobile,* something that more closely simulated an opponent.

He couldn't find anything, so he invented it.

Enter *The Original Profender*.

The Profender is a simulated player on a movable base—arms stretched high over its head—that a coach or fellow teammate controls on the court. It can be pushed forward and backward and raised quickly to attempt to block a shot. It's used to train players to improve their reaction time, aim and other essential skills.

In short, it prepares a player to respond to all the different kinds of adversity they'll face on the court. In fact, the Profender is adversity personified. It's designed to create the feel of a real game while you're training.

It's genius, if you ask me.

Now, when he was designing the Profender, I'll bet Tony didn't see it as anything more than an exceptional basketball training tool.

That's where my vision comes in. Because in my mind the Profender is the perfect symbol for how to keep you on your toes for the game of *life*.

The Profender of Your Mind

You must stand guard at the doorway of your mind.

~ Larry Raskin

Alright. Life is awesome. Every day you wake up, it's a great day and you're seeing that there are *so many* opportunities for success in this world, regardless of your environment or financial situation.

What creates a success story out of a tragedy—or vice versa—is how you handle the Profender of life: adversity.

We've all heard countless stories about a person who has every disadvantage possible. Nothing seems to go right for them. They don't have any help from anyone. Sometimes they rise above their circumstances and sometimes they don't. And, listen, if you've been born into a tough situation, life can seem unbearable.

I get that. I by no means want to minimize these kinds of situations.

But I *do* want to say this: You can accomplish virtually anything in life if you understand and follow the 90/10 rule:

**Life is 10 percent what happens to you
and 90 percent how you respond to it.**

That's *respond.*

Not *react.*

There's a HUGE difference between the two.

Reactions are quick, gut level and require no thinking.

Responses require thought.

Imagine getting up in the middle of the night to use the bathroom. It's dark, and as you make your way across the room you kick a dumbbell you left on the floor. You want to scream in pain and kick the dumbbell again in anger.

That would be reacting. You'd wake up the rest of the house and quadruple the pain in your toe. How smart is that?

Instead you pause, think about it, then suck in your breath, suck up the pain and tell yourself to clean up after working out.

That's a response.

By this point in the book you are far better equipped to respond as opposed to simply reacting to situations as they arise.

But—and this is important—just because responses require *thought* doesn't mean they have to slow you down. Here's where all the training of the mind comes in (and all of your other training for that matter—but we'll get to that).

Even though internally you're responding, to the outside world it'll look like you're reacting, so quick will your responses be. This is the power of training on every level. You've trained so well that your mind can calculate the best response in an instant.

You might hear things like, "That player's so quick on their feet it seems like the game slows down for them."

That's because your responses will become second nature. They won't require an intense and lengthy thought process. Instead they'll be based largely on the training you've already got under your belt.

That's the power of the mind.

I've said already there's really only one thing that you have 100 percent complete control over in your life: the thoughts you allow to stay in your mind.

Notice I didn't say "the thoughts you *let* into your mind." I said *allow* to stay in your mind.

I use the word "allow" because, again, at all times you decide what thoughts get to stay in your mind. Sure, there are times when thoughts are thrust into your mind without your consent. Stuff happens. People say this or that, or your subconscious mind just tosses out something for you to chew on. You see something, hear something or smell something and it triggers a negative thought in your mind.

That's just part of life.

But when this happens, and it will, you have two options:

- Let the negative thought linger while unintentionally consenting to a life of negativity, or
- Utilize your new found mental toughness and push that thought the heck out of your mind. And don't let it back in.

What will you DECIDE to do?

Hopefully by now your choice is clear.

By the way, have you figured out what the true Profender of the mind is?

It's simple: every negative situation you encounter.

That's right. I said *every* negative situation you encounter. Someone tells you you aren't good enough. Your teacher says you can't pass a test. Someone else tells you you'll never amount to anything.

We've all had stuff like that happen.

That's the Profender (adversity) in action. Use it. Overcome it. This is the positive side of the Profender. Everything it throws at us is a seed to plant in the garden of the mind for future growth.

You can learn so much from negative issues that arise. You develop new skills, new powers of making decisions (PEDs), new ways of seeing things. When the pressure's on and you're forced to make the right decision in a practice *or* a real-life situation, there is no other result possible but *improvement*.

Succeed or fail, you learn, and you're the better for it next time around.

FINAL TIME OUT

I'm using my final time out. I'm calling it here because I want you to finish strong. Sometimes, as we near the end of something, we start looking ahead for the finish line before we're there.

So now I'm asking you to buckle down, refocus and finish this game the way you're supposed to. Finish this book with the same enthusiasm and excitement you had when you read the first page.

Make a **P**erformance **E**nhancing **D**ecision now and decide you'll finish with focus and an unyielding passion for success.

"People usually fail when they are on the verge of success, so give as much care to the end as you do to the beginning."

~ Lao Tzu (*Tao Te Ching*)

The Profender of Your Body

You've grown a lot—physically and mentally—since you started reading this book. By now I'll bet you're feeling like an amazing specimen of the human species. You move like a true athlete. You don't compare yourself to others anymore—only to your potential. The compliments are flowing and everyone wants to know what you've done to transform yourself.

You feel awesome, and you should.

But then adversity strikes.

You strain a muscle or twist an ankle. Maybe you really do a number on your body and tear a muscle, ligament or tendon, or even break a bone.

The Profender of the body is injury.

Physical adversity at its finest.

Guess what? Here again, you've got two options: react or respond.

You can sulk, get angry, curse the world, curl up in the corner and talk about how life's not fair.

OR you can do what you've been training for all along. Find the silver lining in the situation.

When adversity strikes, turn tragedy into triumph.

Here's an example. If you hurt your ankle, you can still lift weights with your upper body. You can watch hours of practice film as you go through your rehab sessions. You can visualize more. And remember that study we talked about above that showed mental exercises can help muscles get stronger.

Here's the point: you can *always* find a way to improve, even in the face of the Profender.

It all comes down to how serious you are and how badly you want it. You can't get results and make excuses at the same time.

So decide what you want: results or excuses.

What's the PED here?

The Profender of Your Skills

You are now an outstanding basketball player.

You've developed skills you never dared dream possible because you've followed a proven system designed to produce results. Now you can do the most amazing things on the court— almost effortlessly.

It wasn't that hard was it?

Well, of course it was, but that's why you're here now. You've separated yourself from the masses.

And now, the Profender.

Training time and game time are two totally different animals. Anyone can go through the motions in training and feel great about themselves. They knock down uncontested jump shots as they count down 3, 2, 1 . . . SCORE!

Mentally you feel great, and that's an important part of success.

But the real question is this: can you do it in real game situations when the pressure is on?

If the answer is no, then you must train even harder in practice by making the practice as close to a real game as possible. Training this way will absolutely enhance your skills when the game is on the line.

Using training tools like an actual Profender on the court forces you to do things the right way. When taking a jump shot, you're supposed to *jump*. High. When you set a screen, you're supposed to hold your position until the defender hits into you. When you make a cut, it's supposed to be sharp.

But in training most players just go through the motions and think that they can turn on some magical "game" switch when it's time to really play. They see the likes of Jordan, Kobe, Curry, Durant and LeBron all turn it on when they want to, and then they assume they can be like them.

What they don't understand is that during the game these superstars aren't doing anything different from what they're doing in practice.

They're not turning on a switch.

They're doing what they've trained to do.

What people don't see are the hours upon hours spent not just practicing their craft but *training at game speed*. The superstars use training tools and each other to push themselves out of their comfort zones.

One thing Coach Tony Devine always asks is, "To improve your shot, what's better: taking a thousand shots against air or taking five hundred game-speed contested shots?"

I think that's a rhetorical question, don't you?

If you train for how the game is played, your potential for success multiplies tenfold.

So don't just train.

Play.

Summary

So what have we learned about the Profender?

Although it was created as an amazing basketball training tool, it's a perfect metaphor for a *life*-training tool. No matter how good you are or how well you prepare your mind, body and skills, you're going to get hit with some type of adversity (physical or mental).

When that happens, keep in mind this great Chinese proverb I first heard years ago:

Fall down seven times, get up eight times.

Always remember: **GET UP!**

BEST JORDAN QUOTE EVER

I practice as if I'm playing a game, so when the moment comes in the game, it's not new to me. That's the beauty of the game of basketball, that's the reason why you practice, that's the effort. So when you get to that moment you don't have to think, instinctively things happen.

~ **Michael Jordan**

The Final Buzzer

The Final Buzzer

So there you have it.

We've reached the end of our journey together. You've now got a map to becoming a totally balanced, peak-performing person in all aspects of your life, and you understand the importance of making PEDs every step of the way.

- Was the journey fun?
- Was it all you expected?
- Did you learn anything?

Hopefully your answers are **YES, YES** and **YES**.

My personal goal is to change lives. I believe you achieve that by having fun, meeting expectations and, of course, learning.

I hope you've learned a lot about yourself by reading his book. I know I've learned a lot writing it. What's key now is that we both *keep* learning, keep improving, keep growing.

In the process of writing I realized again what commitment can do for you. I created some excellent habits and removed so many disempowering beliefs that I even surprised myself.

And I learned yet again the main point I've attempted to share with you throughout this book: almost everything in your life, be it mind, body or skills, is totally within your control, once you have developed yourself.

Follow a proven system with dedication and you get results.

It's simple, but not easy.

You won't get there overnight. It takes work and it takes time. Be patient, and let your true potential be seen—by you and everyone else.

I *know* you will amaze yourself.

POST-GAME LOCKER ROOM QUOTE

The problem is not that there are problems. The problem is expecting otherwise and thinking that having problems is a problem.

~ Theodore Rubin

The Post Game Speech

Here's what I want you to do:

Stop reading for a minute and go take a long look in the mirror. Seriously?

Yes. Go. Right now. Put down the book, look at yourself, then come back here and start reading again.

Hopefully after everything we've been through, you'll see what I see when *I* look at you.

Back already? Good.

Okay, here's what I see:

A totally balanced, peak-performing person.

I see someone who stands out from the masses because they have a confidence that has been developed and *earned.*

Their first **P**erformance **E**nhancing **D**ecision—to read this book to the end and *act* on it—has paid off in full.

I see a person who laughs in the face of adversity because they have properly trained their mind, body and skills to accomplish what they need to accomplish. And they've done this by following a proven method of growth.

They have achieved their goals by not rushing things, by putting in the time and effort required to become successful. They understand what it takes to make it to the next level in life and are willing to continue to do it, and to raise the bar once a goal has been achieved.

They see that they have more to offer this world than they ever imagined. They share their secrets of success and help others become successful. And that's the very reason that they continue to grow and contribute.

Finally, they realize that although improving basketball skills is a major component of this book, in the end it really has nothing to do with basketball.

This book is about *YOU. All of you!*

I hope you see all that in yourself.

Because *I* see it in you.

So, congratulations. You've just completed your first course in life training. You now have the knowledge and tools needed for success.

That's the good news.

The bad news? Well, it's not really bad news at all: excuses are no longer an option for you.

Now it's your responsibility to spread the message about **PEDs.**

USE

PERFORMANCE ENHANCING DECISIONS

DAILY.

SHARE THEM WITH EVERYONE.

BECOME A HARD-CORE ADDICT.

GO PROVE SOMETHING!

THE END!

OR IS IT . . .

THE BEGINNING?

Celebrate endings, for they precede new beginnings.

~ **Jonathan Lockwood Huie**

Anthony M. Drago

Anthony offers coaching for groups and in private, one-on-one sessions. He is also available to come to your location and speak to teams, groups, schools, corporations—ANYONE who wants to transform themselves into the person, athlete, student, CEO or teacher they were meant to be.

For more information, contact Anthony at:

amd@anthonymdrago.com
Website: www.anthonymdrago.com

GPS Lifestyle Sports Programs

GPS Lifestyle Basketball Training Clinics

These clinics are unlike anything you've ever experienced. Typically there are Personal Development seminars, Basketball Skills clinics, or Speed, Agility and Quickness training. We break the mold and combine all three in an intense, mind, body and skills boot camp.

GPS Lifestyle Speed, Agility and Quickness Training

SAQ training is vital for any serious athlete. Don't let the basics slide! Learn to reduce the risk of non-contact injuries—one of the most common kind in sports—by learning proper body mechanics and movement patterns.

GPS Lifestyle Personal Development Training

One-on-One Personal Development Training

Many times people prefer a more personal approach to developing themselves. Together, you and Anthony will prepare a personalized plan to help you achieve your goals utilizing a step-by-step process. Figure out what's stopping you from moving forward. Take control of your life and reach your full potential. Can be done over the phone or in person.

Team / Group Personal Development Training

As a coach, it can be hard to get through to your team. Many times you're the only voice of reason they hear. It often helps to bring in a trainer from outside your organization to add a new twist to your training methods. Break through the complacency that can occasionally overtake even the best teams. Work with Anthony to deliver a message so powerful that players will want to run through walls for their teammates, and inject new life into your coaching.

Organization / Company Personal Development Training

The biggest reason companies fail is not because their employees lack skills. It's often because those individuals aren't happy in their jobs. Whether you're the employer or the employee, learning new personal development skills can ramp up your enjoyment of life and work, and re-engage you with everything you do. Let Anthony show you how.

Made in the USA
San Bernardino, CA
22 March 2016